# Framing a Domain for Work and Family

# Framing a Domain for Work and Family

## A Study of Women in Residential Real Estate Sales Work

Carol S. Wharton

LEXINGTON BOOKS
*Lanham • Boulder • New York • Oxford*

LEXINGTON BOOKS

Published in the United States of America
by Lexington Books
4720 Boston Way, Lanham, Maryland 20706

12 Hid's Copse Road
Cumnor Hill, Oxford OX2 9JJ, England

Copyright © 2002 by Lexington Books

*All rights reserved.* No part of this publication may be reproduced, stored in a retrieval system, or transmitted in any form or by any means, electronic, mechanical, photocopying, recording, or otherwise, without the prior permission of the publisher.

British Library Cataloguing in Publication Information Available

Library of Congress Cataloging-in-Publication Data Available

ISBN 0-7391-0367-9 (alk. cloth)

Printed in the United States of America

∞™ The paper used in this publication meets the minimum requirements of American National Standard for Information Sciences—Permanence of Paper for Printed Library Materials, ANSI/NISO Z39.48–1992.

*To the memory of my father, Carl E. Wharton, the first realtor in my life, and to my mother, Trudy, and my daughters, Katrina and Erika*

# Contents

| | |
|---|---|
| Introduction | 1 |
| Part One: Working Full-Time on Their Own Time: The Lure of Independent Contracting | 17 |
| Chapter One: The Nature of Real Estate Sales Work | 19 |
| Chapter Two: Being a Realtor | 37 |
| Chapter Three: Arranging the Workday | 67 |
| Part Two: The Home Is Still Their Domain: Women Work within and outside of Their Family Responsibilities | 81 |
| Chapter Four: Homework: Women as Realtors, Wives, and Mothers | 83 |
| Chapter Five: Real Estate Sales Work as Gender Work | 101 |
| Chapter Six: Good Job/Bad Job: The Perks and Piques of Selling Houses | 117 |
| Conclusion | 135 |
| Appendix | 143 |

| | |
|---|---|
| Selected Bibliography | 149 |
| Index | 157 |
| About the Author | 165 |

# Introduction

> As women's numbers increased in residential sales . . . more female role models demonstrated that selling houses is something women can do . . . After 1971 even women who had never bought or sold a house saw television commercials that featured women selling houses.
> —**Barbara J. Thomas** and **Barbara F. Reskin**, *A Woman's Place is Selling Homes*[1]

> When I first told people that I was taking the real estate course, the attitude was "You're going to get your real estate license? Don't you know everybody has their real estate license?" And then they told me the joke about when you go to the grocery store [and write a check], they ask you for your real estate license because not everybody has a driver's license.
> —**Casey Burns**, seven years experience selling real estate[2]

When you drive or walk down a residential street anywhere in the United States, the chances are good that you will see a "For Sale" sign in front of at least one house. In addition to the name of a real estate company, the sign will usually have a sales agent's name and phone number attached. Very often, that name will be a woman's. Depending on the size of the town or city, you may see the names of a few or many different agents, but once you start paying attention to the names, you will probably find that a high proportion of the agents are women.

I initially became aware of this pattern in 1985 when I was shopping for my first house. Every agent with whom I had contact was a woman. The prevalence of women was particularly interesting to me because my father had been a real estate agent and broker in the 1960s, and I could recall only one woman among his colleagues. I began to observe realtors' advertisements and to wonder if the field had undergone a gender shift in the interval between the 1960s and the 1980s. Then in the late 1980s, I heard about Barbara F. Reskin's and Patricia A. Roos's work on occupational resegregation, with several case studies of specific occupations, including real estate, that had shifted in gender composition in recent years. Roughly six percent of the U.S. labor force is employed in real estate and finance. Eighty-two percent of real estate salespersons sell residential property, and over fifty percent of residential salespeople are women.[3] Women have constituted a high percentage of realtors only since the 1970s. I wanted to know more about why this increased participation of women had occurred and why the field began and continues to appeal to women.

My interest in this topic led me to study women realtors from a sociological perspective. I had two goals in this study. First, I wanted to understand the experiences of women like those whose names I saw on so many "For Sale" signs: how they have made real estate their domain, how they arrange their work, what they like about it, and what they find distasteful or uncomfortable. Second, I wanted to place the work within the larger context of women's lives, as a case study of the factors that women must negotiate in integrating their work and family obligations.

Many questions concerning the structure of real estate sales work and how the women organize their work occurred to me as I began this study. Those questions included the following: What is the relationship between real estate agencies and individual salespeople? Do real estate agents work for a company or are they self-employed? Do agents work solely for sales commissions or do they also receive a salary? What are the expenses involved in selling real estate? How does an individual become qualified for this job? What makes this occupation attractive to women? Is it more attractive to some categories of women, such as married or single women, women with or without children, older or younger women? What are the advantages and disadvantages of the work for women in these various demographic categories?

Other questions concerned how the women realtors view their work: what are the reasons they find themselves in this occupation in the first place? What do they see as the positive and negative aspects of the experience? Do the women perceive gender as being related to their selection and performance of the job? Do they believe that the fact that they are women has any bearing on their work? How do family responsibilities relate to this job? What connections do women with children see between their role as mothers and their role as realtors? How do they fulfill the obligations of each role? Do they see their paid work as compatible with their family life? How closely do the women's experiences match their expectations about the work and its compatibility with their family obligations? These are the questions that constitute the basis of this study.

Although I started with the perception that residential real estate sales work was becoming a "woman's job," that the field was resegregating as increasing numbers of women entered it, I have come to question whether that process is actually occurring. It did seem at the time of Reskin's and Roos's study that real estate was a good example of the process of occupational "tipping," a term borrowed from studies of racial desegregation in housing. Residential tipping occurs when a formerly segregated neighborhood begins to desegregate and, as minority families increase their presence, the majority population leaves in increasing numbers until the neighborhood becomes resegregated as a minority area. In applying the concept of tipping to gender in occupations, as a predominately male occupation opens to women and increasing numbers of women enter the field, men leave it and it becomes a predominately female occupation. Thus, if real estate sales work followed that pattern, it would go from a male occupation to one defined as women's work. However, over the past decade, the proportion of women to men has stabilized, and real estate sales may end up as an example of genuine integration in an occupation.

Regardless of whether or not residential real estate sales tips over into a resegregated occupation, my interest continues to focus on women's experiences in this field. I have found that even in an occupation with high percentages of both women and men, gender is a salient and significant factor in determining how workers experience the job.

## Women and Work

The study of women in real estate sales work contributes to an understanding of women's work in the late twentieth and early twenty-first centuries. While the general topic of women and work is receiving increased sociological attention, most of the research concerns domestic work, pink- or blue-collar work or the career professions.[4] Relatively little research focuses on white-collar, paraprofessional, service occupations.[5] This category includes real estate, insurance and other forms of commissioned, direct sales work, as well as accounting, consulting, and small business entrepreneurships. Increasing numbers of middle-class women are developing this kind of work into careers that give them a sense of autonomy in their work and an expectation of compatibility with their family obligations. It is expedient, therefore, to understand the nature of this type of work, the factors that make it attractive to women, and the significance of gender, race, and class to the workers' experiences.

Women workers share some aspects of work with all women, although they also experience differences based on whether they are middle or working class, and whether they are white, African American, Hispanic, or members of another racial ethnic group. Membership in a privileged group often means that one is oblivious to the significance of that privilege. Thus, white middle-class men may argue that race, class, and gender are irrelevant to their work experiences. In the same way, white middle-class women may not see any ways that race and class have affected their work lives although they may be aware of gender as a variable. Minority racial ethnic women, on the other hand, are more likely to believe that race is a factor in their work experiences. Similarly, poor and working-class women and men may see their class position as significant in determining the kinds of work that are available to them.[6] My analysis focuses almost exclusively on how gender affects work experiences, and vice versa, although where possible I have indicated class and race effects.

Gendered practices infuse the workplace and are in turn shaped by the nature of the work itself. Assumptions about women and men are reflected in the ways that people go about their work and other daily activities. As these ways of doing things become habitual, they help to reproduce differences between women and men.[7] For example, men in the skilled trades emphasize their strength and knowledge of machinery as masculine traits that make men more suitable than women to these kinds of jobs. In fact, however, technology has made strength mostly irrelevant and women are as capable as are men of learning how to operate the machinery.[8] But because men and women believe that these traits are masculine, society encourages boys to become physically strong and mechanically adept. In the same way, people believe that women are more nurturing and encourage girls to enter the caring professions.[9]

The previous examples of the skilled trades and the caring professions both refer to occupational categories that are still highly segregated by gender and in which resistance to gender integration remains strong. Thus, they illustrate how gender is sustained in long-accustomed practices (i.e., when I conjure a mental image of a skilled trades worker—a plumber, carpenter, or roofer—I see a man, even though I am aware that women may also fill these jobs. When I meet a woman who is in a trade such as plumbing, I see her as "masculine" in some ways—her attire, physical bearing, demeanor. She is breaching boundaries, whether I salute or censor her for it).

The gendering that occurs in real estate sales work is different. Here, the image of the worker is not gender-specific. When I think of a realtor, I am as likely to envision a woman as I am to envision a man. The nature of the work is neither "masculine" nor "feminine" in the current period (although thirty years ago, I would have pictured a man as a realtor, and fifteen years ago, I might have been more likely to picture a woman as a realtor). Yet, as I shall argue in chapter 5, the women realtors themselves have reconstituted gender as significant to their work.

A second issue in the study of the role of gender in work experiences is the way that different frames of reference have been applied to women and men. The job model, which focuses on workers as independent and separate from other aspects of their lives outside of work, is often the starting point in research when men are the subjects. The job model ignores the impact of family responsibilities on work experiences. When men succeed or fail at work, the characteristics of the job become the most significant explanation. Any family dynamics that affect the worker's job experience are overlooked.

The gender model, which views the family as the primary determinant of work decisions, is more often the framework when women workers are the objects of research.[10] The gender model ignores or minimizes the importance of working conditions in shaping the worker's experiences. When women succeed or fail at work, it is the characteristics of her family life—the presence or absence of children and their ages, the presence or absence of a spouse and his support or lack thereof—that become the explanation. The work conditions that make a job a good or bad "fit" are ignored.

A similar framework, which Anita Ilta Garey terms the "orientation model,"[11] seeks to explain women's experiences as the result of individual priorities: women are either "work oriented" or "family oriented," and those of the first orientation are assumed to be more focused on their work and therefore more "successful" in its performance than those of the family orientation. Work and family compete for women's attention in a zero-sum orientation. The "mommy track" was a proposal that evolved out of this perceived dichotomy. "Family-oriented" women could take the mommy track and not compete with or be evaluated in comparison to work-oriented women or (all) men.[12] As Garey points out, men are not linked to the same dichotomy. A "family man" is both work- and family-oriented. Part of his obligation as a father is to provide economic support to the family. Thus the concept "working father" sounds redundant, while "working mother" connotes a woman who is combining two roles.

These models need to be combined in order to gain a more comprehensive understanding of women's lives. Family and work configurations shape both women's and men's everyday lives. Women don't want to choose between work and family; they want and usually need to combine the two realms.

Garey employs the metaphor of "weaving," as a process and a product, to analyze the relationships between women's work and families. Through the activities of working and mothering, women produce a life pattern composed of the connections among the various aspects of their experiences:

> As a process, weaving is a conscious, creative act. It requires not only vision and planning, but also the ability to improvise when materials are scarce, to vary color and texture in response to available resources, to change direction in design, and to splice new yarn. As a product, a weaving reveals both grand patterns and minor designs. It reveals the connections between pattern changes and how what has come before is linked to what follows, and it reveals the richness or thinness of the materials used.[13]

To an extent, the weaving metaphor describes my approach to the women realtors. I wanted to study how they "wove" together their family responsibilities and their work of selling homes. I started with an assumption that women with children at home would find real estate sales work appealing because they would see it as a viable way to accomplish their family work at the same time as they were providing economic support. They could be available to their children and other family members at varying times, according to the changing needs of the family. Again drawing on my own experiences, my father usually came home and ate lunch with us when I was a child, and he could take time to attend our school activities. On the other hand, he was away from home many evenings after dinner, and sometimes had appointments on weekends to show houses.

Thinking back on these taken-for-granted arrangements, it initially seemed apparent to me that real estate sales work is compatible with having a family, and I wondered why most of the realtors during my childhood were men. I did not initially think about all of the work that my mother, as a full-time homemaker, did that gave my father the means to weave together his work and family experiences: she was there when he had appointments, took care of all of the shopping, cooking, doctors' appointments, laundry, and other tasks of family living. A woman realtor without a full-time household assistant would not have the same flexibility that my father had.

So I liked the imagery of women weaving a pattern of homemaking and selling that I would explore in this study. But as I looked at my data again and again, it became apparent that I did not have a nice, neat picture of a whole cloth composed of work, family, and the other components of a woman's life. Instead, I had focused more on the framework—the loom so to speak—that women had constructed in order to produce their own particular patterns of living as mothers and workers.

Christena E. Nippert-Eng provided another building block in my analysis. She applies what she calls boundary theory to a complex analysis of how people cognitively negotiate the relationship between home and work.[14] She finds that people define and combine "home" and "work" in a wide variety of ways, from total integration of the two realms to complete segmentation of one's work and family lives. Characteristics such as autonomy and flexibility of scheduling of work, as well as household composition and attitudes toward work influence where the individual falls on this continuum. For example, people who "love" their work are more likely to bring it home with them than are those who view their work only as a means to support themselves and their families.

Boundaries shift over time and vary at both the macro level—from one society or social group to another—and the micro level, between individuals and families. For example, there was no boundary between work and home in preindustrial societies, where the family was the unit of production and labored in their own fields and shops. By contrast, work and home became separate "conceptual territories"[15] during the early stages of industrialization, when "work" became defined as what one earned a wage to do and "home" became the domain of unpaid, reproductive labor for the family. In postindustrial societies, the boundaries are again more flexible, as more people work at or from their homes. In each of these periods, the boundaries are cognitive and relative: e.g., the housewife works at home at the same time as her labor is discounted as not "work."

Although Nippert-Eng finds gender to be mostly unrelated, I wanted to explore this issue further. It seemed probable that women with children at home would prefer work that had flexible boundaries, and would in any case integrate their family and paid work obligations as fully as possible.

Thus, I have borrowed from these two theoretical concepts—weaving and boundary work—to develop my own focus on the framework that makes possible a satisfactory combining of work and family, within the context of gendered practices. The image here is of the framing for a building under construction: what are the shapes and materials that make the strongest domain in which women can raise their children, develop a rewarding career, and fulfill all of the obligations of their personal and public lives in satisfying ways. Specifically, by looking at real estate sales work, a better understanding emerges of what features of *both* work and family are mutually compatible. I do this by examining the working conditions and the family responsibilities of women realtors.

## The Participants

For this study, I conducted in-depth interviews with thirty women from seventeen real estate firms. I used a "snowball" sampling method, meaning that I started with the names of five women in five different agencies. These women's names came from friends or acquaintances who knew that I was looking for women selling residential real estate and who, preferably, had families that included children of preschool or school age. From those five contacts, each person interviewed gave me the names of two or three other women to contact.

Because racial diversity in the sample was important to me, I began requesting names of African American women after the first few referrals included only white women. The final group of respondents included twenty-five white women and five black women. While I would have preferred a more racially diverse and balanced sample, the proportion of black realtors to white realtors in the area of the study is even lower than the one to five ratio of this sample.[16] Furthermore, the questions I asked did not result in different descriptions by white and black women of the work of selling houses. The principal difference discussed by black and white realtors concerned their own consciousness of race as a factor in their work, and that is discussed in chapter 2.

I was less aware of socioeconomic class as a variable during the interviews, but certain differences in the respondents' experiences are class related or can be explained by their class position. These are also discussed in the second chapter.

All of the respondents lived and worked in the Richmond, Virginia, metropolitan area. They ranged in age from twenty-nine to forty-eight years, with a median age of forty. Twenty-four women were married and six were single (divorced, separated, or never married). The age and marital status distributions of these respondents may not be typical of women in real estate, because I was interested particularly in women with children at home, and this factor probably skewed my sample toward younger, married women. Indeed, my preliminary reading indicated that this demographic group was ideally suited to the work (see chapter 4). Interestingly, a recent (1999) survey by the National Association of Realtors revealed that the average Realtor®[17] is a fifty-two-year-old, married, white woman. This finding raises concerns for the National Association, because it verifies the Association's impression that new agents are not entering the field in as large numbers as expected. Only six percent of sales agents are younger than thirty, while forty-eight percent are fifty years or older.[18] The Association's findings reassure me, however, about the representative age of my sample, since in 1990 the average realtor would have been in the age range of this group of respondents.

My focus on the specific category of women realtors with children at home stemmed from the fact that I wanted to know how women combined family obligations with this type of work. As a result of this focus, I tried to select women who had at least one child younger than twelve years of age, assuming that they would have the most demanding family obligations. That is, they would at least have to arrange for after-school and weekend child care if they worked during those hours.[19]

All but one of the respondents had children. Eleven of them had one child each; sixteen had two to four children each; and two women had five children each. The children ranged in age from five months to twenty-four years, with a median age of ten years. All of those women whose children were older than twelve years had been selling real estate since their children were younger than twelve. Thus, they were able to compare their work/family arrangements now with then, to describe how their work and family constructions had changed as their children became more independent.

Although educational achievement was not a criterion of selection for my sample, all but two of the women I interviewed had some education beyond high school. Thirteen had completed one to three years of college; ten were college graduates, and five had masters' degrees. These numbers are similar to the national figures for 1999, when all realtors had finished high school, eighty-seven percent had some college education, forty-three percent had completed a bachelor's degree, and an additional eighteen percent had done graduate work.

Prior to entering the real estate field, the women had held a wide range of jobs. Ten of the women had held clerical or lower-level-management positions in government agencies or private corporations. Seven of the women had been public school teachers; three had been social workers, and three had held other sales jobs. Nine of the thirty women, including some of those included in the occupations listed above, had been full-time mothers and homemakers immediately prior to beginning to sell real estate. (A table of demographic characteristics is available in the Appendix.) In the membership of the National Association of Realtors, management and sales, teaching, administration, and homemaking are the most common prior full-time careers for women.

Additional characteristics of the respondents included the numbers of years of experience and the types of real estate agencies, based on size and whether the agency was independently owned or part of a national franchise or affiliation. The numbers of years of experience the women had in real estate sales ranged from one to fourteen, with a median of five years. The seventeen agencies included thirteen that were independently owned and four that were franchises or affiliates of nationally owned companies. The size of the agencies ranged from five to four hundred salespeople, with a median size of twenty salespeople.

## The Research

I conducted open-ended interviews with each woman, usually at her office, although occasionally at her home or a coffee shop. The interviews were tape recorded and later transcribed verbatim. The interviews lasted from one-and-a-half to three hours and included detailed descriptions of what attracted the women to the job, how closely their experiences matched their expectations, their work structures, how they did their work, and what they found satisfying and frustrating about their work. (A copy of the interview schedule is included in the Appendix.)

I interviewed only one woman who was leaving her job as a realtor, and this was because she had been a site agent for a new housing development that had been completed. She also had recently separated from her husband and was not earning enough money to make it economically viable to continue.[20] With that one exception I ended up interviewing women who planned to stay in this occupation, at least for the time being, although there were variations in their prognoses for the future. While I asked each of the women I interviewed to include the names of women who had left the field, none did so. Each woman said that she did not know anyone who had left the field or did not know what had become of those who had.[21] As a result, I can address only the experiences of real estate sales work for those who are involved in it. It is probable that women who dropped out of this occupation would have very different perspectives on their experiences.

This research began in 1990, with the interviews taking place from January through March. As I began to organize my material for this book, I wondered how the women whom I interviewed in 1990 were faring by 1998. How many of them were still in this occupation? If they were still selling houses, were they with the same firms? How had their work experiences changed as their family situations developed and changed? Real estate is a field with a high turnover rate, and I was curious about how closely my subjects fit the general pattern. More broadly, I was interested in the stability of occupational placement for women employed in white-collar service work.

To answer these questions, Katherine Willis, a sociology student at the University of Richmond, and I went back in the spring of 1998 to try to find the thirty women whom I had interviewed in 1990. We found twenty-four of them in the local directory of realtors. The remaining six were not listed and could not be located, either by calling the firms with whom they had been affiliated in 1990 or by telephone directory. One of those six had been planning to quit selling real estate at the time of the original interview; apparently the others have left the area or changed their names (perhaps through marriage or divorce), or have unlisted phone numbers.

Of the twenty-four women that we found, eleven were still affiliated with the same firm, although two of these firms had changed names and been involved in a merger with another firm. The remaining thirteen women had changed firms. These findings confirm the fact that real estate has a fairly high rate of turnover. If the six women whom we did not locate have all left the field, they represent twenty percent of the original respondents. Of the twenty-four remaining women, fifty-four percent have changed agencies.

For the follow-up interviews, we designed a schedule that focused on the women's current work situation and allowed us to make comparisons to their answers in 1990. Only two of the women remembered being interviewed in 1990, and we did not remind anyone of the responses they gave then. Therefore, we are confident that the women were not making any attempt to reconcile their answers with their original responses. Katherine met each woman at her office and tape-recorded the interviews, which lasted from thirty minutes to an hour. We both listened to the taped interviews, and then she transcribed them verbatim. Throughout the book, I make comparisons between the two sets of data.

## The Organization of the Book

The book begins with a specific description of the work involved in selling residential real estate and moves to a more general analysis of issues currently facing working women. The book is divided into two parts. Part 1 looks at residential real estate sales work as an example of occupations that employ independent contractors. The issues of affiliating with a company, obtaining necessary training and licensing, and setting one's work schedule are typical of this type of work.

To understand the women's experiences, chapter 1 explains the nature of the work. The occupation may be defined as contingent work, interactive service work, emotional labor, and a pseudoprofession. In each of these senses, the job represents a growing proportion of occupations. This chapter also includes a brief history of women's entry into the field and their increasing presence in residential sales work over the course of the twentieth century.

Chapter 2 describes the experience of being a realtor: the job requirements, the procedure of joining a firm, negotiations for commissions, and practices for attracting customers. The second chapter also discusses various types of relationships between realtors and their customers, and the significance of socioeconomic class and race.

Chapter 3 discusses how the women arrange their work daily and weekly. As independent contractors, they are solely responsible for determining their own work schedules, but in order to complete a sufficient volume of business to meet their sales goals, they must work steadily and efficiently. Thus, each realtor devises a work pattern that best suits her needs and preferences.

Part 2 continues the examination of this occupation, but steps back further to explore some dimensions of work that are common to women in general: How do women accomplish the tasks of their paid work while also maintaining a satisfactory personal life? How does being a woman affect one's work experiences? What criteria lead women into certain occupations? Chapter 4 looks at how the women arrange work and family responsibilities, the "boundary work" that occurs between these two areas of their lives, and the effects of flexible scheduling on these arrangements. Respondents' work lives are shaped by the nature of the work, their partners' schedules, their gender ideologies, and the availability of other types of house help.

Chapter 5 considers the issue of gender as it relates to the work, examining how the women perceive gender as significant in their sales experiences. This includes ways that the women see gender as an asset, as a liability, or simply as making a difference in their experiences. The meaning of gender for the respondents is a fundamental element of their individual identities. This meaning illustrates the theoretical perspective of recent scholarship, which posits gender as a socially constructed and fundamental category by which the members of a society organize social relationships, both individually and structurally.[22]

Chapter 6 assesses the work in terms of its attractiveness: the respondents' assessments of what drew them into the field initially and whether these expectations were realistic. If not, then what other factors keep them in this occupation? The respondents discuss the desirable features of the work as well as what they would prefer to change about it. This chapter describes the framework that enables compatibility between work and home.

Finally, chapter 7 summarizes the findings and draws some conclusions about the interactive relationship between people's work, gender, and family lives.

# Notes

1. Barbara J. Thomas and Barbara F. Reskin, "A Woman's Place is Selling Homes: Occupational Change and the Feminization of Real Estate Sales," in *Job Queues, Gender Queues: Explaining Women's Inroads into Male Occupations*, ed. Barbara F. Reskin and Patricia A. Roos (Philadelphia, Pa.: Temple University Press, 1990), 217.

2. All names of realtors are pseudonyms.

3. Barbara F. Reskin and Patricia A. Roos, *Job Queues, Gender Queues: Explaining Women's Inroads into Male Occupations* (Philadelphia, Pa.: Temple University Press, 1990).

4. For examples of research concerning pink- or blue-collar work, see Greta Foff Paules, *Dishing it Out: Power and Resistance among Waitresses in a New Jersey Restaurant* (Philadelphia, Pa.: Temple University Press, 1991); Ellen I. Rosen, *Bitter Choices: Blue Collar Women In and Out of Work* (Chicago: University of Chicago Press, 1987). For domestic work, see Mary Romero, *Maid in the U.S.A.* (New York: Routledge, Chapman, and Hall, 1992). For the career professions, see Ruth Carter and Gill Kirkup, *Women in Engineering* (New York: New York University Press, 1990); Sheila K. Collins, "Women at the Top of Women's

Fields: Social Work, Nursing, and Education," in *The Worth of Women's Work: A Qualitative Synthesis*, ed. Anne Statham, Eleanor M. Miller, and Hans O. Mauksch (Albany: State University of New York Press, 1988), 187-201; and Cynthia Fuchs Epstein, *Women in Law* (Garden City, N.J.: Anchor Books,1983).

5. Some of the research which has focused on this category includes Helen Lawson, *Ladies on the Lot: Women, Car Sales, and the Pursuit of the American Dream*, (Lanham, Md.: Rowman & Littlefield Publishers, 2000); Nicole W. Biggart, *Charismatic Capitalism: Direct Selling Organizations in America* (Chicago: University of Chicago Press, 1989); Maureen Connelly and Patricia Rhoton, "Women in Direct Sales: A Comparison of Mary Kay and Amway Sales Workers," in *The Worth of Women's Work: A Qualitative Synthesis*, ed. Anne Statham, Eleanor M. Miller, and Hans O. Mauksch (Albany: State University of New York Press, 1988), 245-264; Betty Beach, *Integrating Work and Family Life* (Albany: State University of New York Press,1989).

6. See, for example, Evelyn Nakano Glenn, "The Social Construction and Institutionalization of Gender and Race: An Integrative Framework," in *Revisioning Gender,* ed. Myra Marx Ferree, Judith Lorber, and Beth B. Hess (Thousand Oaks, Calif.: Sage Publications,1999), 3-43.

7. Joan Acker, "Forward," In *Gendered Practices in Working Life*, ed. Liisa Rantalaiho and Tuula Heiskanen (New York: St. Martin's Press, 1997), ix-xi.

8. Kath Weston. "Production as Means, Production as Metaphor: Women's Struggles to Enter the Trades" in *Uncertain Terms: Negotiating Gender in American Culture*, ed. Faye Ginsburg and Anna Lowenhaupt Tsing (Boston: Beacon Press, 1990), 137-151.

9. Francesca M. Cancian and Stacey J. Oliker, *Caring and Gender* (Thousand Oaks, Calif.: Pine Forge Press, 2000).

10. Kivimaki, Riikka, "Work and Parenthood," in *Gendered Practices in Working Life,* ed. Liisa Rantalaiho and Tuula Heiskanen (New York: St. Martin's Press, 1997), 83.

11. Anita Ilta Garey, *Weaving Work and Motherhood* (Philadelphia, Pa.: Temple University Press, 1999).

12. Felice N.Schwartz, *Breaking with Tradition: Women and Work, The New Facts of Life* (New York: Warner Books, 1992) proposed two career tracks for women although it was the media who dubbed her family-oriented option the "mommy track."

13. Garey, *Weaving*, 14.

14. Christena Nippert-Eng, *Home and Work: Negotiating Boundaries through Everyday Life* (Chicago: University of Chicago Press, 1996).

15. Nippert-Eng, *Home and Work*, 277.

16. A recent survey by the National Association of Realtors found that 95 percent of realtors are white, while the remaining 5 percent combines African American, Latino, and Asian American agents (*Richmond Times-Dispatch*, October 3,

1999, 1G).

17. *Richmond Times-Dispatch*, October 3, 1999, 1G.

18. It was the respondents themselves who determined this age as my cut-off point. All of the women with children twelve years of age or younger said that they made arrangements so that the children were not left home alone. Arlie Hochschild found a significant number of parents who said that their children, ages six to thirteen, stayed alone routinely, and that it was the professional and managerial parents who did so more often than the minimum-wage parents. Hochschild cites national surveys that estimate that there were twelve million "latch-key children" in 1994 (*The Time Bind: When Work Becomes Home and Home Becomes Work*, New York: Time Warner, 1997): 233-234. Among my respondents, women with children older than twelve years sometimes left them at home when the women worked, especially if they were going out to show a house or deliver a contract and expected to be gone only a couple of hours.

19. Realtor® is a registered trademark for members of the National Association of Realtors.

20. This woman had been making enough money to live on while the housing development was still in the building stage. She had made more money than her husband, in fact. But, at least partially because she had not branched out beyond the site, her income had fallen drastically in the past year.

21. I found this a curious phenomenon. The turnover rate in residential sales is high, and yet none of the women could identify any former colleagues.

22. Sandra Harding, *The Science Question in Feminism* (Ithaca, N.Y.: Cornell University Press, 1986); Mary Hawkesworth, "Confounding Gender," *Signs: Journal of Women in Culture and Society* 22, no. 3 (spring 1997): 649-685.

# Part One

# Working Full-Time on Their Own Time: The Lure of Independent Contracting

## Chapter One

# The Nature of Real Estate Sales Work

> A quiet revolution in the workplace has been underway for nearly three decades. Five significant changes define this revolution: (1) in the way employers deal with uncertainties, both in product demand and labor supply; (2) in personnel policies and training methods; (3) in compensation and benefit policies; (4) in the way a significant portion of the labor force enters the job market and acquires skills and experience; and (5) perhaps most importantly, in the nature of the employment relationship itself.
> —**Donald Mayall**, "Temporary Work and Labor Market Detachment: New Mechanisms and New Opportunities"[1]

> My real estate image was there was a realtor when I was growing up who was very successful. I come from a very middle-class environment. And she had a big car, and a nicer house than we did, and she seemed very independent, self-sufficient, had a good sense of humor, and everybody knew her. And I guess when I thought about real estate I thought about her.
> —**Beth Tripp**, three years' experience selling real estate.

Sociologists and other scholars of work have devoted much attention in recent years to the changing nature of work. The most significant changes have resulted from the shift from industrial production to technological production, service provision, and information processing.[2] While millions of workers are still engaged in blue-collar assembly lines, manufacturing is moving to other countries with lower wages, or being replaced by technology. Increasingly, workers must look to other forms of employment, primarily involving the manipulation of information rather than the manipulation of materials.[3] One of the most rapidly growing areas of work is that of "high touch" occupations in "people services."[4]

Deindustrialization and technological changes free more and more workers from the space/time constraints of traditional work arrangements. Through telecommunications they can work where and, to a large extent, when they choose. Alternately, some types of service work require meeting customers in their homes or at other locations away from the work site. For this growing segment of the workforce, a central office/workplace is no longer necessary, and more autonomy in shaping one's work environment is possible. Boundaries between work and other areas of one's life become flexible, even ambivalent. Race, class, and gender characteristics become more or less important depending on the amount of face-to-face interaction involved in the work. Telecommuters are physically invisible to their employers and their customers/clients. On the other hand, interactive service workers are in direct contact with customers and their physical characteristics may be significant in these interactions.

Women workers, who often have demanding family responsibilities that they must coordinate with their paid work, have been receptive to these new work arrangements. Autonomy in determining one's work schedule and the location of the work are particularly attractive to women with families. Since sixty-eight percent of women with children under the age of eighteen years and sixty-one percent of married women with a spouse present in the home are in the paid labor force, there is tremendous pressure to adapt working conditions to family needs and vice versa.[5]

In many ways, real estate sales work represents the changing nature of work in the United States at this time in history. It is an example of a job that requires its practitioners to work away from a central office, to spend a great deal of time on the telephone and on the road. The business of selling real estate is conducted increasingly via computers. House listings are posted on the internet. Mortgage rates are available from all over the country. Individual realtors develop their own home pages. Electronic mail serves the same role as voice mail in allowing messages to be exchanged among all concerned parties when they are not in at the same time. The work itself does not seem to have any relationship to the gender or race of its practitioners. People can become successful realtors regardless of their religion, marital, and parenting statuses, or other social categories. The boundary between work and home is blurred: the realtor's work *is* homes, and s/he is therefore constantly addressing other people's home needs. Further, the realtor often goes directly from her/his home to meet clients at a house for sale, and takes phone calls at home.

Realtors have more apparent autonomy than do hourly wage assembly line or salaried office workers. Realtors can determine their own hours of work and take time off for other activities. They can work by telephone and computer from their cars and homes while they cook, watch their children, or drive carpool. But they have little protection in the form of disability pay or medical leave and cannot be certain of their income from month to month. They must pay their own social security and taxes, and any medical insurance or retirement fund they may have. Realtors are in a sense entrepreneurs, since they are technically self-employed, although legally they are required to work under the protection of a broker.

Real estate sales is a type of service work, specifically interactive service work, meaning that it requires workers' direct involvement with customers or clients.[6] As work in industrial production declines, the number of people employed in service occupations increases. Predictions are that by 2005, more than eighty-one percent of the U.S. labor force will be employed in service industries.[7] This category includes clerical work, counseling, entertainment, finance, food service, fund-raising, health care, insurance, public administration, sales, teaching, trade, and transportation.[8] People, as service recipients, become the "raw materials" of the work process.[9] As customers, clients, patients, respondents, passengers, or prospects,[10] they must participate in interactions to accomplish the work of providing a service. Service workers and service recipients negotiate interactions through social exchanges, rituals, and manipulation.[11] Much of service workers' success depends on how well they handle those interactions. How they present themselves matters as well as the "product" they are selling. The worker's physical appearance becomes a significant factor in customers' responses (the realtor's presentation of self is discussed in chapter 2).

Thus, a home buyer or seller is the service recipient whose reactions determine the realtor's success or failure. The realtor must interact with the home seller/buyer in ways that convince the latter that the product (the home for sale) is desirable and the worker (the realtor) is competent and trustworthy.

Real estate is, further, a form of contingent work, defined as jobs lacking long-term contracts or guaranteed minimum hours. Contingent workers include part-timers, temporaries, and independent contractors, and represent an increasing number of workers. Their numbers are predicted to grow to perhaps one-half of the U.S. workforce in the next few years.[12] Most of the recent attention to contingent work has focused on its disadvantages for the worker, which include a lack of health care and pension benefits, sick leave, vacation pay, workers' compensation, unemployment insurance, and social security. Many workers are reluctant participants, whose jobs have converted to contingent status as employers seek to cut costs and make their workforce more adaptable to fluctuations in demand. About two-thirds of contingent workers are women, and the majority of them would prefer a permanent, full-time job.[13] However, there is also a segment of the workforce that prefers or chooses contingent work. These are most likely to be independent contractors, who may earn more per hour than salaried workers although they also lack employee benefits. Real estate salespeople fall into this latter category, independent contractors who find advantages in their contingent status.

Selling houses is also a type of emotion work, as agents work with clients in finding and/or selling housing, since it involves managing the feelings of the workers and the customers.[14] Successful sales work requires making customers "feel good" about the transaction, meeting the customers' demands and enhancing the appeal of the commodity (emotional labor is discussed further in chapter 6).

In short, the realtor, like the "new worker" in general, is an independent contractor, involved in interactive service work. S/he relies increasingly on technological assistance, with the tantalizing potential of succeeding in his/her own business, but with the accompanying cost of having little or no job security.

To relate this occupation back to the "quiet revolution" in the workplace, all five changes outlined by Mayall (see quotation at the beginning of this chapter) can be demonstrated in real estate: First, real estate sales work has experienced changes in the ways employers deal with uncertainties, both in product demand and labor supply. In contrast to traditional employers, brokers deal with uncertainties in the housing market by shifting the burden to realtors. As independent contractors, realtors pay the costs of maintaining themselves in the business when sales are low.

A second change in the workplace relates to the shifting nature of personnel policies and training methods. Again, as independent contractors, realtors are responsible for their own training prior to licensing, and must be licensed before joining a company. Companies sometimes pay for additional training by sponsoring in-house classes. These are most common in large firms, for motivational courses and to update the sales force on the latest techniques or changes in legal requirements. For obtaining specialized certifications or to brush up on information before being recertified, however, realtors usually have to take classes at their own expense.

Third, the new workplace is characterized by changes in compensation and benefit policies. Real estate sales work includes no paid leaves, vacations, or other benefits, and no contract of employment. Realtors must pay their own income taxes, social security, disability, health, and life insurance premiums. Job security is an irrelevant concept since, as independent contractors, realtors have no employment contracts. They would not be "fired" because the company is not an employer in this sense, but they could lose their office space or access to the company's logo at any time. Brokers do have an interest in attracting and retaining good realtors, however. To that end, they offer incentives in the form of office support and sliding commissions that increase the realtor's percentage as sales volume and/or longevity increases (see the next chapter for a fuller explanation of this process.)

As a fourth change, workers enter the job market and acquire skills and experiences differently than they did in the past. Rather than advertising job openings, the recruitment of realtors is an informal process. A broker or realtor from one firm will meet a realtor who is looking for a company with which to associate, because s/he has just obtained certification or is unhappy with her/his present company. Conversely, a realtor might approach a company that has a good reputation, or attract attention with a high sales volume. At any rate, the realtor is then invited to "try" the firm.

Finally, the new workplace includes changes in the nature of the employment relationship itself. The realtor's relationship to the job of selling homes focuses primarily on the customers/clients, not on the broker as an employer. The broker's interest is in keeping productive realtors affiliated with the company and enhancing their earnings. Thus, the broker and the realtor are more like partners than like employer and employee, although of course the realtor does not share the company's profits as a true partner would do. As will be discussed in the next chapter, I expected realtors to resent brokers as exploiting them by taking part of their sales commission, but was unable to find any sentiment of that sort. Instead, realtors said that they appreciated their brokers' expertise and protection.

## The Development of Real Estate as an Occupation

Helping people find housing has probably been a pastime for as long as there have been exchanges of property. One can only speculate as to how ancient humans negotiated the acquisition and disposition of living quarters. Perhaps the earliest sociological analysis of real estate as an occupation was completed in 1928, when Everett C. Hughes studied the Chicago

Real Estate Board.[15] Hughes characterized real estate agents as "casuals," meaning that they were people who did not view their work as a career or even as permanent employment. Instead, they had a temporary (casual) relationship to their work, in terms of both time and capital investment.

The next sociological examination of real estate sales occupations appeared in 1977. This was a case study of one large company in Canada. The author, J. D. House, characterized the real estate agent as "one of the last of a declining social type, the individual entrepreneur."[16] While it appears that this prediction was inaccurate since individual entrepreneurs have increased as a category of workers in the 1990s and are expected to continue to grow into the next decade, the study did provide valuable information on the role of the residential real estate agent. By the 1970s, the real estate agent had moved beyond the earlier concept of "the casual" and become an "expert negotiator,"[17] mediating between amateurs buying and selling houses.

The structure of residential real estate sales work changed significantly in the 1960s and 1970s. At that time legislation allowed real estate firms to shift salespersons from the status of employee, with a salary and varying benefits in addition to commissions on each home sold, to that of independent contractor, with pay based solely on commissions. One effect of this shift was to reduce the risks to the broker imposed by inexperienced salespersons. Whether the salesperson is more or less productive does not affect the broker as greatly as if salary and benefits were involved. At about that same time, national franchise firms such as Century 21 were developing and slowly making inroads into markets that had been dominated by locally owned companies and independent brokers. This development meant that opportunities opened for large numbers of new salespeople.

Real estate salespeople routinely refer to themselves as professionals, but the concept of professional work has been reserved traditionally for occupations with more stringent entry requirements, such as law, medicine, and teaching. Today, however, increasing categories of workers call themselves professionals: termite inspectors, house painters, even house cleaners. What, then, is a profession? How is a profession different from other jobs? And where does real estate fit into the picture?

A profession may be defined partially as an occupation with high status and specialized knowledge.[18] Also, an occupation gains the designation of a profession if it provides services that are highly valued by the members of a society, but are not easily accessible. Thus, medical doctors provide knowledge of healing and disease that is not available to lay people without specialized training and state licensing. Even if individuals were to read and educate themselves in the latest medical knowledge, they could not become doctors without formal educational credentials.

By these criteria, then, it would seem obvious that the occupations of house painters and maids are not professions. It is more difficult to determine whether selling real estate is a profession. Salespersons must be licensed by their state, according to the particular regulations of that state. In most cases, agents must work under the supervision of a broker, or have a broker's license themselves. Brokers are also licensed by their states, and may either operate their own business or work under another broker. Brokers are responsible legally for the actions of the agents who work under them.

All of the women interviewed for this study were Realtors®, which is a registered trademark for real estate sales agents who have joined the National Association of Realtors and subscribe to its code of ethics. In order to become a Realtor®, each of the women had gone through a training period in preparation for taking the state licensing examination. The training ranged from several weeks of classes once a week to two weeks of classes every day. A few took a course at a local community college or university; others took courses offered independently by for-profit operations. Regardless, after passing the class, everyone had to take the state licensing examination. In addition, most of the subjects had gone on to acquire further training and technical designations, such as Certified Site Agent (CSA) or Certified Residential Specialist (CRS). A few had completed the requirements for a broker's license, which include several of the above types of designation, a specific amount of experience as a sales agent, further classes, and an additional licensing examination.

Recently, the state had passed a new requirement that all salespeople had to renew their licenses every three years by taking a refresher course and an exam. Many also took classes on specific issues, such as writing sales contracts and qualifying customers financially. Most agents also took motivational classes periodically, to keep up their enthusiasm for the work and learn new strategies for increasing their sales.

Other criteria of professions are that they are occupations whose practitioners possess autonomy, authority over clients and other workers, and a certain degree of altruism. Salespeople, as independent contractors, are autonomous and have authority over clerical helpers and support staff. Companies and local real estate boards display altruism by participating in community projects and charitable fundraisers. For example, the local board has participated in Habitat for Humanity projects, both by raising money and by working on the actual labor of building houses.

Finally, a profession is usually widely respected, conferring high status on its members. Being a realtor does not typically confer high status, although some realtors, as well as some housing contractors, may have achieved relatively high status in their communities. Gaining acceptance as a profession also involves some public relations work. That is, for the members of an occupation to persuade outsiders that they are professionals, their work must be perceived as desirable, a preferred type of work. For this acceptance to occur, the work must fulfill an important need of the society, a need that can only, or best, be met by the members of that occupation. By requiring any person who negotiates the sale of real estate other than his or her own property to be licensed by the state, the need for realtors becomes increasingly widespread. And realtors are quick to argue that they do a much better job of selling houses than do individual homeowners (see the disparaging description of "FIZBOs" in chapter 2).

In short, the field of residential sales is becoming increasingly regulated and professionalized, requiring specialized and abstract knowledge. It is no longer possible to enter as a "casual" or amateur. On the other hand, it certainly is easier to enter this field than it is to become a doctor, lawyer, or teacher. Perhaps it would be more accurate to claim that real estate is engaged in a *process of professionalization*, emulating a profession in an effort to improve the standing of the occupation. The process of professionalization involves moving from part-time to full-time work, requiring formal training and credentials, and having a national organization that will create a code of ethics and work to achieve legal recognition of the occupation as a profession.[19]

For most realtors, sales work has become a full-time job. Although few who are presently engaged in the occupation have received their training in a college-level program, many believe that this will become necessary in the near future, and they already must complete training approved by the state board. The National Association of Realtors represents the interests of the occupation and strives to achieve the rights and privileges of a profession for its members. And, finally, the National Association of Realtors has created a code of ethics to ensure that its members behave in a professional manner.[20]

For realtors, as well as people in many other occupations, being classified as professionals is important to workers' self-perception. It may also influence how much respect outsiders accord workers in a field, and perhaps even increase the amount of compensation that an occupation is able to command. Realtors talk about behaving "professionally." They want the public to perceive them as responsible professionals, and they maintain a professional appearance in their demeanor and in the ways that they conduct their work. For example, one of the women interviewed said that she gets frustrated when other realtors do not seem to take the profession seriously:

> I think it's really important to make our industry into a profession. And it really bothers me that people think they want to just do it part time. They don't know how to do business like it ought to be done. I would like for more women to look at it as I'm sure the top producers do, we look at it as our business. This is our business, and we run it like it's our business. My wish would be for more women to look at it that way, rather than just to think they're going to dabble in it.

Many of the same women acknowledge, however, that the general public does not accord them this status. As Tonia Marks, a realtor with eleven years of experience, told me, "The image of realtors is, well, maybe a step up from the used car salesman." Tonia believed that part of the reason for this public disdain was that entry requirements had been too lenient in the past. She hoped that the national and state licensing agencies would continue to enforce more stringent entry requirements:

> It helps us realtors. We work so hard to keep our image high, and to let people know that we subscribe to the national code of ethics. And as we increase the educational requirements, it's just going to keep increasing the image.

Some respondents felt that the training standards were still not sufficient to make the job a profession. For example, Ginger Allen had been an elementary school teacher before becoming a realtor, and felt that in comparison to the qualifications required for a teaching certificate, those required for even the "advanced" designations of real estate sales work were too lenient:

> I've been busy with [obtaining titles in] the real estate field itself and I am somewhat disillusioned. It took me seven years to go through college, because I went at night and weekends and lunch hours, and then to find out that to get a GRI [Graduate Realtor® Institute] simply meant three weeks of class attendance under an informal atmosphere. I really questioned what was a GRI or a CSA. I have a CSA, Certified Site Agent, and that took two days. And after you've been through the academic pressures that I went through in the past, that just doesn't seem like a great deal of time. It doesn't mean any more money. In fact, a lot of people who've made the

most money have put it off and then go back and get the CSA or the GRI simply because it's what you do.

Ginger's assessment of the training criteria was more critical than that of some of the realtors who had no other forms of semi professional or professional experience to which they could compare their real estate training. Others felt very intimidated by the entry requirements and said that they had heard that a high percentage of applicants failed the licensing test. These latter respondents were more likely to refer to real estate sales work as a profession, while Ginger and others like her who disparaged the entry requirements did not use the term.

## The Changing Gender Composition of the Residential Sales Force

Women have been involved in real estate sales work since at least the 1920s. In 1928, Hughes described women in the occupation as prototypical "casuals," implying that they were relatively new to the field:

> It is as the sub-division salesman [sic] that the woman finds her place in the real estate business. The characteristic thing about the woman who looks for a job is that she hasn't one already. She is the casual par excellence. Like the hobo, she is likely not to want her job long, or to devote herself to it too completely. Some crisis may throw her into the labor market, to grasp at any passing driftwood.[21]

Although the situation for women in real estate has changed dramatically since 1928, Hughes's own example belied his stereotype of the woman realtor as only temporarily committed to her work. He cited a woman, whom he described as typical, who was a widow and worked fulltime as a salesperson, building her clientele and establishing a place for herself in the Chicago real estate market. Clearly, she was not a "casual par excellence," nor was she any less devoted to her job than her male counterpart.

The 1928 study did not explore the issue of gender further, except to refer to an article in the *Chicago Tribune,* "announcing the belief that women salespeople usually are better equipped with that elusive and indefinable something commonly known as tact than are the male members of the selling force."[22] Whether or not the real estate industry and the general public perceived women as possessing this quality, they still did not make up the majority of salespeople until some forty to fifty years later. The proportion of women to men in real estate shifted dramatically, beginning in the 1960s. Currently, men continue to constitute the bulk of managerial (broker-manager) positions and to dominate nonresidential specialties, but the majority of salespersons at the residential sales level are women.

In the 1980s it appeared that residential real estate was becoming increasingly defined as "women's work" through a process of *gender resegregation*. In this pattern, an occupation that has been dominated by one gender becomes more accessible to the other gender and as members of the second gender increase their numbers, the first gender gradually leaves the field, perceiving it as no longer suitable work for them. Thus, a job that had been viewed as a man's field would gradually come to be defined as a woman's, or vice versa. The process of resegregation usually occurs in the following pattern: Rapid growth of a field, because of changes in population or technology, creates a labor demand greater than can be met by the existing pool of workers. Wages and other benefits do not increase with the increasing labor demands, while at the same time other fields are competing for the same labor pool and offering better incentives. Concurrently, the labor pool is expanding as other categories of workers enter the labor force—due to factors including immigration and ideological changes in the definition of workers suitable for an occupation.

The typical pattern of gender resegregation is exemplified by the changes that occurred in the nineteenth century in the clerical and teaching professions. Both changes were accompanied by adjustments in the rhetorical justifications of the work as appropriate for women.[23] For example, public-school teaching, which had previously been defined as a male occupation, opened to women in the latter half of the nineteenth century in this way: (1) There was a substantial increase in the demand for teachers as a result of population growth, an increased commitment to universal education, and a desire to decrease the number of students per class. These changes meant that for teaching to have remained a male profession, the percentage of all male workers engaged in teaching would have had to increase. (2) At the same time as the demand for schoolteachers increased, school boards were unwilling to increase wages to attract males. School boards required a "native-born middle-class appearance and behavior"[24] and good moral character, but did not pay enough to support a family with middle-class standards. (3) The teaching profession was changing in ways that men did not find desirable: schooling became more regulated and teachers lost much of their former autonomy. Meanwhile, new and more attractive opportunities were opening for men in business and industry. (4) The American society in the nineteenth century witnessed a major ideological campaign in favor of women's entry into teaching, as women began to move out of the home into the paid labor force. Each of these changes facilitated the entry of large numbers of women into teaching. Gradually, teaching became "women's work," particularly at the lower levels of public education. The same general process occurred in clerical work, as the demand for "typewriters" (a term that referred originally to the people operating the new typing machines) outstripped the supply of male workers.

Parallel changes occurred in the second half of the twentieth century in the real estate field, and propelled increasing numbers of women into residential sales. There are four major structural reasons that residential real estate sales became more accessible to women beginning in the 1970s. First, the shift of salespersons from the status of employee to that of independent contractor altered the pay structure from salaries to commissions and therefore reduced the risks of employing inexperienced salespersons who might be less productive. Second, economic fluctuations made commission-based earnings less attractive to primary wage earners and resulted in large declines in the number of men in residential real estate sales, at the same time that large numbers of married women with children were entering the labor force. Concurrently, the rapid growth of national franchise firms such as Century 21 allowed openings for many new salespeople, and these franchises focused their recruitment efforts on women.

Finally, men in real estate shifted to nonresidential specialties and left the field of residential sales more open to women than at any previous time in history.[25] Men moved out of residential real estate as the rewards declined relative to occupations requiring similar qualifications. Opportunities opened in other areas of real estate—managerial positions as brokers/owners in their own firms, commercial sales, development—as well as in other occupations, which provided greater autonomy, and higher income and status than did residential sales. So far, women have not moved on in the same way. Research on women's mobility patterns in other occupations suggests that the explanation for this lesser mobility lies in the choice of reference groups: women compare themselves to other women and find their work preferable to the alternatives available.[26] They perceive fewer alternatives for themselves than do men. Felicia Lee expressed this perspective:

> It's the only thing I could do that I could make enough money to make it worth my while. A woman without a college education has very limited

choices, even less than a man with similar education.

All of these factors led analysts to expect the resegregation of residential real estate sales work.[27] In the case of race relations, true integration occurs only if the races achieve togetherness and blacks enjoy real autonomy as individuals and as a group. Mere desegregation does not result in increased personal and group autonomy. Desegregation often leads to "white flight" as white people move out of a neighborhood when blacks move into it. Thus, a neighborhood becomes resegregated as black.

Barbara Reskin and Patricia Roos use the theoretical models of racial desegregation to analyze the patterns of women's inroads into occupations traditionally defined as men's work. However, the last stage of the typical pattern of occupational resegregation has not occurred in real estate. The proportion of men to women shifted dramatically as huge numbers of women entered the occupation and men moved into other specializations or other kinds of work. But a large number of men stayed in residential sales, and significant numbers of men continue to enter the field. In fact, the trend toward greater proportions of women slowed in the late 1980s, and dropped from a high of sixty-four percent in 1987 to fifty-six percent in 1996 and fifty-eight percent in 1999.[28] For the time being, at least, it appears that women will continue to constitute a majority of the residential sales force, but men will also define the work as appropriate for themselves. Thus, it seems that this occupation has become *de*segregrated. However, Reskin and Roos argue:

> Occupational resegregation is an almost inevitable outcome of substantial occupational desegregation. Thus, what appeared to be integration was sometimes only a temporary stage in a longer process of resegregation.[29]

They examined whether women integrated all levels of the occupations or if gender segregation persisted within the occupations. They also questioned whether the post-1970 integration of their case study occupations was merely a stage in a process of their resegregation as female. They conceptualized three forms of occupational desegregation by gender: genuine integration, ghettoization, and resegregation. They found ghettoization, in which men and women perform different jobs within the same occupation, to be the modal form in their case study occupations, including real estate sales. Specifically, ghettoization of real estate sales occurred horizontally, as women came to constitute the majority of residential salespersons and men moved into commercial sales, and vertically as men retained the majority of brokers' positions while women stayed in the position of salesperson.

Looking at these patterns in the 1990s, however, the pattern of ghettoization and/or resegregation is harder to trace. By 1999, forty-five percent of brokers were women while men constituted forty-two percent of full-time sales agents. It would seem equally plausible to argue that this occupation is achieving genuine integration as it moves into the twenty-first century. It will be interesting to watch what happens in the next decade or two, before any conclusions can be made about the gender composition of the field.

## Routinization and Scripting

Finally, in characterizing real estate sales work, it is important to address the issues of routinization and scripting. Routinization refers to the process of organizing work so that the worker has no control over the way the work proceeds. All such decisions are made by managers and engineers and the worker simply follows a prescribed "routine."[30] Scripting involves the development of specific verbal and nonverbal routines for workers to follow in interacting with customers. In highly routinized jobs, employers construct scripts for their employees based on assumptions about what behaviors customers prefer. Thus, in fast food sales and airline attendants' training, programs focus on teaching workers routines for handling most interactions with customers/clients. Some of the assumptions that guide the design and enactment of these routines are gender-related, concerning definitions of how women and men should behave. For example, Leidner found that the training for insurance agents emphasized determination, aggressiveness, persistence, and stoicism as attributes important for success, and characterized these as manly traits.[31]

Real estate is somewhat less routinized than insurance, and much less so than fast food sales, although it is clearly headed in the direction of greater routinization, as indicated by the growing numbers of regulations and training seminars geared toward reducing the ambiguities of selling real estate. Currently, though, real estate is less scripted by employers than are many other sales jobs, due in large part to the nature of the relationship of sales agents to their brokers: Agents are required by law to work for brokers, but they maintain the status of independent contractors. Thus, realtors have more autonomy than do salaried employees.

In summary, real estate sales work is a quasi-professional, interactive service occupation, performed by independent contractors. It represents a revolution in the nature of work, as increasing numbers of workers move from the relative security of long-term employment in salaried jobs to the uncertainties of contingent work. On the plus side, such jobs give workers greater autonomy and the possibility of earning more money based on their own productivity. On the negative side, there are no company-supplied benefits and no minimum salary to fall back on when productivity slumps.

The field appears to be a blossoming example of true occupational integration, as the proportion of women to men in the field stabilizes at roughly three to two. Nevertheless, the workers perceive gender as an important variable in how they experience and perform their job. The next chapter describes the experience of being a realtor, and how the occupation is structured as independent contracting work.

# Notes

1. Donald Mayall, "Temporary Work and Labor Market Detachment," in *The New Modern Times: Factors Reshaping the World of Work*, ed. David B. Bills (Albany: State University of New York Press, 1995), 163.

2. Kai Erikson, "Introduction," in *The Nature of Work: Sociological Perspectives*, eds. Kai Erikson and Steven P. Vallas (New Haven, Conn.: Yale University Press 1990), 1-15.

3. R. Alan Hedley, *Making a Living: Technology and Change* (New York: Harper Collins, 1992), 5.

4. Lisa D. Brush, "Gender, Work, Who Cares? Production, Reproduction, Deindustrialization, and Business as Usual," in *Revisioning Gender*, eds. Myra Marx Ferree, Judith Lorber, and Beth B. Hess (Thousand Oaks, Calif.: Sage Publications, 1999), 162.

5. Dana Dunn, *Workplace/Women's Place: An Anthology* (Los Angeles: Roxbury Publishing Company, 1997), 9.

6. Robin Leidner, *Fast Food, Fast Talk: Service Work and the Routinization of Everyday Life* (Berkeley: University of California Press, 1993).

7. Leidner, *Fast Food, Fast Talk*, 28.

8. Randy Hodson and Teresa A. Sullivan, *The Social Organization of Work* (New York: Wadsworth Publishing Company, 1995).

9. Hodson and Sullivan, *The Social Organization of Work*, 2.

10. Robin Leidner, in *Fast Food, Fast Talk,* 3, points out that the terms used are problematic:

There is no commonly used term for the nonemployees involved in service interactions. I will frequently use the inelegant term "service recipients" for this generic category, since, unlike "customers" or "clients," it can include people involved in noncommercial or nonvoluntary interactions. It is not an ideal term, however, since some types of participants, such as survey respondents, do not receive any service.

11. Leidner, *Fast Food, Fast Talk*.

12. Karen Judd and Sandy Pope, "The New Job Squeeze: Women Pushed into Part-Time Work," *Ms. Magazine* 4 (May/June 1994): 86-90; Anne Polivka and T. Nardone, "On the Definition of 'Contingent Work,'" *Monthly Labor Review* 112, (1989): 9-16; Barbara Reskin and Irene Padavic, *Women and Men at Work* (Philadelphia, Pa.: Temple University Press, 1994).

13. Judd and Pope, "The New Job Squeeze," 86.

14. Arlie Hochschild, *The Managed Heart: Commercialization of Human Feeling* (Berkeley: University of California Press, 1983).

15. Everett C. Hughes, *A Study of a Secular Institution: The Chicago Real Estate Board* (Ph.D. Dissertation, University of Chicago, 1928). 146.

16. J. D. House, *Contemporary Entrepreneurs: The Sociology of Residential Real Estate* Agents (Westport, Conn.: Greenwood Press, 1977), 20.

17. House, *Contemporary Entrepreneurs*, 3.

18. Hodson and Sullivan, *The Social Organization of Work*, 132.

19. George Ritzer, *Sociological Beginnings: On the Origins of Key Ideas in Sociology* (New York: McGraw-Hill, 1994); Harold L. Wilensky, "The Professionalization of Everyone?" *American Journal of Sociology* 70, no. 2 (September 1964): 137-158.

20. Carol S. Wharton, "From Casuals to Careers: The Professionalization of Real Estate Sales Work" in *Current Research on Occupations and Professions: Jobs in Context: Circles and Settings*, vol. 10, ed. Helena Z. Lopata (Greenwich, Conn.: Jai Press, 1998), 115-134.

21. Hughes, *A Study of a Secular Institution*, 150.

22. Hughes, *A Study of a Secular Institution*, 150.

23. L. M. Fine, *The Souls of the Skyscraper: Female Clerical Workers in Chicago, 1870-1930* (Philadelphia, Pa.: Temple University Press, 1990); Barbara F. Reskin and Patricia A. Roos, eds. *Job Queues, Gender Queues: Explaining Women's Inroads into Male Occupations* (Philadelphia, Pa.: Temple University Press, 1990); Myra H. Strober, "Toward a General Theory of Occupational Segregation: The Case of Public School Teaching," in *Sex Segregation in the Workplace: Trends, Explanations, and Remedies*, ed. Barbara F. Reskin (Washington, D.C.: National Academy Press, 1984), 144-156.

24. Strober, "Toward a General Theory," 148.

25. Barbara J. Thomas and Barbara F. Reskin, "A Woman's Place is Selling Homes: Occupational Change and the Feminization of Real Estate Sales," in *Job Queues, Gender Queues: Explaining Women's Inroads into Male Occupations*, Barbara F. Reskin and Patricia A. Roos, eds. (Philadelphia, Pa.: Temple University

Press, 1990), 215.

26. Andrew Abbott. "The Sociology of Work and Occupations," in *Annual Review of Sociology*, vol. 19 (1993): 187-209.

27. Barbara F. Reskin and Patricia A. Roos, "Occupational Sex Segregation: Persistence and Change," in *Job Queues, Gender Queues: Explaining Women's Inroads into Male Occupations*, Barbara F. Reskin and Patricia A. Roos, eds. (Philadelphia, Pa.: Temple University Press, 1990), 25.

28. National Association of Realtors, "The Data Bank," *NAR Membership Survey 1999*, http://nar.REALTOR.com/research/papers/member//text.htm (January 11, 2000).

29. Reskin and Roos, *Job Queues, Gender Queues*, 25.

30. Leidner, *Fast Food, Fast Talk*, 28.

31. Training techniques reflected a "spirit of jousting" in which agents were taught to challenge customers:

Virtually every step of the interaction was understood as a challenge to be met: getting through the door, making the prospect relax and warm up, being allowed to start the presentation, getting through the presentation despite interruptions, overcoming prospects' objections and actually making the sale, and perhaps even increasing the size of the sale (Leidner, *Fast Food, Fast Talk*, 203).

Training for agents in this insurance company included elaborate descriptions of typical situations and appropriate responses.

## Chapter Two

# Being a Realtor

There are three types of interactive service work in which the success of the work depends on the quality of the interaction, and therefore on the personal attributes of the worker.... [In the third type] the interaction is a crucial part of the work process even though it is not part of a product being sold or provided. The success of salespeople, fund-raisers, bill collectors, and survey interviewers depends on the workers' ability to construct particular kinds of interactions.
—**Robin Leidner**, *Fast Food, Fast Talk: Service Work and the Routinization of Everyday Life*[1]

I think most people think it's very easy, you make a lot of money, and you don't have to work real hard. You're floating people in and out of these lovely, beautifully decorated homes, and it's so much fun to see them. Well, beautifully decorated homes are few and far between, and it's very grueling when you're with an out-of-town buyer for three or four days and they want to see everything, and it's up and down two-story colonials. You know what they're all like; you've been in them sometimes a hundred times before, but they need to see them. It's hard and you're tired when you get home.
—**Pamela Rice**, eight years' experience selling real estate.

As discussed in the previous chapter, the nature of real estate sales work has changed in recent years and the procedures for entering the field have become more rigorous. This chapter examines the experience of being a realtor, including affiliating with a specific company, earning compensation by commission, finding and keeping customers, and establishing a niche in the market. The description of these processes serves as a case study of the steps involved in doing interactive service work as an independent contractor.

## Joining a Company

Although real estate agents are independent contractors, by law they must have a broker's license or work under the supervision of a licensed broker. Salespersons who have a broker's license may start their own independent agency; those who do not have their own broker's license must affiliate with a company. Several of the respondents had earned or were in the process of earning their broker's licenses, but only two of them planned to start their own companies. The rest saw the broker's license as a further step in their professionalization, but did not want to leave the protection of a larger company or take on the responsibilities of managing a company.

Typically, a company provides office space, telephones and other office equipment, and limited clerical support. Salespersons share office duty and often work cooperatively in showing and promoting each other's listings, although only the listing agent and whoever makes the sale will share the agent's commission, while another percentage of the commission goes to the broker. More rarely, usually in cases of site agents working exclusively in a new housing development, agents work as employees of a company, meaning that they are paid a salary and benefits. In 1999, three percent of Realtors® were employees, compared to ninety-seven percent who were independent contractors.[2]

Brokers or companies do not *hire* real estate agents. Instead, the process of affiliation consists of becoming acquainted with different firms, talking to the brokers/managers and perhaps some other agents associated with those firms, and choosing the firm that best suits the individual agent's preferences. In 1996 the National Association of Realtors (NAR) conducted a survey of real estate agents to find out how agents select a firm. The NAR found that the following ten attributes, in order of importance, were cited as determining factors in choosing a firm: (1) the company's image in the marketplace, (2) the office support staff, (3) computer access to Multiple Listing Services (MLS) provided by the company, (4) the company's market share, (5) the advertising provided by the company, (6) the company's referral network affiliation, (7) sales manager support, (8) franchise affiliation, (9) company-provided education and training opportunities, and (10) company-prepared marketing materials.[3]

While I did not ask my respondents to assess these attributes specifically, each one came up in at least a few answers to my question of what attracted them to their present company. The company's image, or reputation, was a major reason for choosing to affiliate. Respondents also frequently cited the NAR's ninth and tenth reasons—training and educational opportunities, and a company's marketing materials—as significant in their decisions. However, they also mentioned a few other reasons for joining a company. Some of the respondents said that they had joined a company because its owner/manager approached them and asked them to join. In some cases, they had been with another company previously and become dissatisfied with it. The following response, by Elaine James, expresses the most rational and deliberate pattern of choosing a company:

> After I got my license I interviewed, which I would recommend any new person do—in other words, they're not interviewing you, you're interviewing them—and find where you'd be most comfortable. I think I did four or five companies, and I came here. Number one [reason], I had a good friend here that I had a lot of respect for, who'd been in the business at that time for five years. Secondly, I thought this company had a tremendous training program, which when you're brand new, the course you take to get your license has nothing to do with real estate. Truly, it doesn't prepare you for anything. And I felt that this company had a real good training program. And third, I guess, was proximity to my home. It was only five or six minutes away from where I lived. I've moved now, but it's still not that far away. [Finally,]a lot of agents move around a lot, and it seemed like the agents here had stayed close, had roots, and I felt like there must be some reason.

Thus, Elaine's reasons for selecting her company included having a friend at that office, valuing the training offered, the office being conveniently located for her, and a sense that other agents were content there. She had been with this company for six years and felt that her selection method had resulted in a very satisfactory choice. She was, however, rather unusual in being so systematic in her decision making. A more common response to why someone had chosen a particular company was simply that a friend was affiliated with it, or the broker/manager was a personal friend, as in the case of Cara Lange:

> [The husband and wife who own the company] are very close personal friends. We like the same type of homes. It just depends on the circle of people we travel in.

Cara's answer emphasized the personal friendship she had with the owners/managers of her company, but she alluded to another frequent reason for selecting a company. A particular agency was more amenable in some respect with the specific interests or needs of the respondent. For Cara, the company represented her interest in a distinct niche of the housing market, i.e., the "type of homes," by which she meant expensive, custom-built houses in a specific residential area. For others, a company might be compatible with their individual needs. For example, when Sandra Berry wanted to get started in real estate, she couldn't afford to give up a regular paycheck:

> I decided that I was going to get into real estate but my needs were different [from other realtors'] because we didn't have the income, first of all, to hire a full-time sitter and to pay all these expenses and wait several months before the first commission checks came in. So I decided, I had heard that some of these big builders hire their own employees and pay them a salary to work in the model and sell homes. And I started pursuing that angle. I called the sales manager for one such builder and he offered me a job at [a new housing development site]. However, they were not set up to have me as their employee. I had to be licensed, hang my license with [a specific firm] because the builders were under contract with them, to sell all their homes through them. So that's how I got started with this company. The good thing about that was that they paid all my expenses, all my realtor's dues, they did all the advertising. I didn't have any expenses. I worked three days during the week, and I worked every weekend. So that helped me get started.

After working as the site agent under these conditions, Sandra eventually moved full-time into regular real estate sales work as an independent contractor, still affiliated with the company that she had been under contract with on the building site.

Other respondents described their reasons for changing companies after they had been affiliated with one firm. Again, this often happened because they became friends with people in another company, or grew dissatisfied with their original company as their experience grew and/or their needs changed. In the following example, both of these factors led to a change of affiliation for Tonia Marks:

> I was really unhappy with my situation where I had been for about six years. The company had made a lot of changes and it was affecting me financially. So, because I was unhappy I was starting to put my feelers out. And I was at a cocktail party that a builder was having, and I had had dealings with a couple of the other agents from here, and one of the owners of this company was on a committee [with the local Association of Realtors] that I chaired. I had never met her business partner, but at this party I saw them [the two partners] and jokingly I said, "When are you all gonna open up a Southside office?" And they said, "Well, we have to talk to our banker." That was their response. We just let it go. And that's something you usually don't do, out in the open. If you're going to change companies you generally keep it quiet until you do it. Well, the next day I had a committee meeting, and when it was over, [the first owner] said "I'd like to talk to you. Yesterday you asked us for a Southside office. We found one. Now when are you coming to work with us?" And that's what did it!

Tonia's explanation sounds as if the opportunity was entirely serendipitous, but in fact she was already dissatisfied with her situation and she knew one of the owners of the prospective company. Apparently, they also knew her reputation and were eager to recruit her once she expressed an interest. Other respondents said that they selected their present company because of its reputation, its commission split policy, the office equipment (such as computers) available, or the other amenities provided.

In addition to these reasons for joining a particular company, as business via the internet has increased continuously, a company's presence there and ability to assist agents in establishing themselves electronically has become more important as part of the third factor, access to Multiple Listing Services. By 1999, seventy-five percent of NAR members were associated with companies that had a World Wide Web page (see below for further discussion of the uses of computers in selling real estate).[4]

Companies don't advertise openings; indeed, there seem to be no set number of agents in most companies. Size might be determined by available space—the number of individual offices, or the number of desks in a common room. As Elaine James explained:

> It's not like there are a certain number of slots available and you have to wait for one to open. There are certain guidelines set by the Board of Realtors that companies, brokers, have to meet. [For example,] one phone can only be used by two agents. So you couldn't have, say, 10 phones and 50 agents. They don't have to provide an office for each agent. I happen to have an office with two other agents. We each have a desk, and two phones between the three of us. But I've run into situations, agencies, where there was one big room and a lot of phones and desks.

There is a high turnover rate in this business, both in terms of people entering and leaving the field altogether and in people switching companies. Respondents insisted that switching companies was fairly easy to do, and so commonplace that there were rarely any hard feelings. The major requirement in switching seemed to be that an agent cannot take her listings or her customers to another company, although the latter would be harder to enforce. Tonia Marks explained:

> You have to close out all your listings with a company. Any ongoing sales you can keep until they close, and then you get paid. Any listings would stay with the company. So it's prudent to dissolve all your business before you leave.

Most of the switching occurs as a result of an agent's preference for a new setting. As independent contractors, agents are not "fired" by companies, although some companies require a minimum level of sales in order to provide the office amenities. Agents who don't meet that minimum might be asked to leave or, more often, would feel more subtle pressure in the form of loss of collegiality or otherwise being shut out of communication channels. None of my respondents had experienced a situation in which they felt that the company wanted them to leave. Instead, those who had changed companies had done so at their own initiative.

Whether it is choosing the first firm with which to affiliate or deciding to move to another firm after working in the field, the selection process is largely a matter of realtors' individual needs and preferences. This freedom is one of the advantages of their autonomy as independent contractors.

The process of choosing a company with which to affiliate is probably similar for other kinds of independent contracting that require affiliation with some form of licensed agency. In other cases, the company plays a more direct role in recruiting salespeople. For example, Amway and Mary Kay are direct sales organizations in which the agents must buy products from the parent company and then sell those products to the public. There is no licensing requirement, but the company makes its products available only to people who have gone through its training process and who meet certain criteria. The salespeople then turn around and recruit other salespeople who buy the product from them, in a pyramid fashion.[5]

Other kinds of independent contracting do not require such affiliations and the individual can set up her/his own business. For example, a carpenter might set up a home repair business simply by placing an ad in the newspaper and/or handing out flyers or business cards.

## Negotiating Compensation

As independent contractors, realtors' compensation must be based on their sales. The Internal Revenue Service has strict guidelines for determining the status of independent contractors, based on the Tax Equity and Fiscal Responsibility Act (TEFRA) of 1982. This act requires that salespersons be licensed real estate agents who have a written agreement with their broker stating that for federal tax purposes they will not be treated as employees. Compensation may not be based on the number of hours worked but on sales or other output. Thus, the commission earned on each sale is the only source of income for the vast majority of real estate sales people who are independent contractors.[6]

Before beginning this study, I was aware that the usual sales commission on residential real estate was six percent of the sales price, and I assumed that meant that the real estate agent who sold a house received the entire six percent on each sale. However, I quickly discovered that the system is much more complex than that. While it is true that six percent is the standard commission on residential sales, it is not always the rate. A recent article in a local newspaper explained that commissions are negotiable by law in some states, including Virginia, and the real estate board "does not fix, control, recommend, suggest or maintain compensation rates or fees for services to be rendered by members."[7] The board is careful to state this as policy to avoid any suggestion of price-fixing or violating antitrust regulations. The form used by agents in listing a property contains a blank for the agent to fill in a commission percentage after negotiating with the sellers.

Furthermore, whatever the percent, that amount is divided in a variety of ways by different companies and even within the same company. It is also sometimes the case that a seller might negotiate a lower commission when listing her/his house, or accept a lower offer from a buyer in exchange for a lower sales commission for the realtor. In any event, the commission must be divided between the listing agent (the agent who "lists" the house, meaning obtains the initial agreement with the seller and advertises the house) and the agent who actually sells the house (the agent who handles negotiations with a prospective buyer). This division is usually fifty percent of the commission to each agent's company. One respondent, Deborah Engels, explained the process:

> Let's say that the listing fee is six percent, and it's listed by XYZ real estate company, and I have a prospect I take in and I write the contract. So I've participated for half of that, so our company gets three percent, which is

based on the sales price. So three percent of the price, not the listed price but the sales price, goes to my company. Out of that, I get my commission. And the commission split for each individual depends on how much money you made the year before, or the month before, or whatever.

The most variation occurs in the way agents split the commission with their brokers. The simplest split would be fifty-fifty, meaning that the broker and the agent each receive fifty percent of their company's share of the commission. Thus, the listing agent's broker and the listing agent, the selling agent's broker and the selling agent would each receive one and a half percent of the total six percent commission. However, this type of split is actually fairly rare. More common is the graduated split: the more sales an agent makes the higher the splits. In its 1999 membership survey, the NAR found that eighty-two percent of sales agents receive a commission split, with a median starting split of fifty-five percent and a median year-end split of sixty percent. For most of my respondents, also, the broker/agent split was never fifty/fifty. In the following example, presented by Ginger Allen, the split is reset every year:

> The more income you make during the year, the higher your splits get, and you [could] go all the way up to ninety/ten [agent/broker's shares]. Once you have made thirty thousand [dollars] of income, you're at seventy percent. Then every year you start back at seventy, so you don't have to go back [further than seventy-thirty]. Generally, we start at sixty/forty, but if an agent would rather take a fifty/fifty split and have the company pay a certain part of their expenses, they have that option.

The expenses that a company might pay in exchange for a higher percentage of the sales commission include advertising costs and office services such as clerical assistance and copying expenses. Agents who negotiate a higher percentage of the commission often have to pay for their own advertising, copying, and postage.

It would be important to know whether gender plays a role in the negotiating of compensation. The respondents did not think so. They contended that men and women were assessed by the same standards, with the main criterion being their annual sales volume and earned income. The NAR is silent on this topic, not maintaining statistics on the correlation between gender and compensation. However, it is a plausible correlation, since brokers and agents negotiate these commission splits on a one-to-one basis, at the time the agent joins a firm and at regular intervals thereafter. It is certainly possible that a male broker negotiating with a female agent might be more or less flexible than with a male agent, and vice versa. On the other hand, the agent's sales record would give her/him more or less leverage, regardless of gender.

Although none of my respondents worked for a company that did not require a split, several described an arrangement offered by one company, which is part of a national franchise. In this arrangement, the agent pays the company a monthly fee and then is entitled to keep one hundred percent of his/her commissions:

> [The agent] pays [the company] one thousand dollars a month or something like that. And then you still have to pay for your advertising and everything—your stationery and all the office expenses. That's just to give you a roof over your head. But that one thousand dollars a month is tax deductible, it's a business expense. So if you're a big producer and make one hundred percent of your commission it would be good.

In this type of arrangement, the "roof over your head" refers to having office space and more importantly, to using the company's logo in advertising. The 1999 NAR survey found that eighty-two percent of sales agents worked for a percentage commission split. Another thirteen percent worked for one hundred percent commission, while one percent received a straight salary, two percent received a salary plus a share of profits, and two percent received a commission plus a share of profits. The combined three percent who received a salary or a salary and a share of profits would not fall under the TEFRA definition of independent contractors but would instead be employees.

In exchange for their share of the commission, brokers provide legal protection for agents (although agents also must carry their own "errors and omissions" insurance[8]), as well as office space, clerical assistance, telephones, and a variety of other material benefits. However, as indicated by the quotation above, some companies may require agents to pay at least partially for even these services. The general rule seems to be, the more amenities provided by the company, the higher the broker's share of the commission, and vice versa. The following is Lana Kight's assessment of the broker's contribution:

> He provides the administrative staff, the computer system, microfilm for research on city and county properties. The signs, the name, reputation. If we run a full-page ad in the front of the Real Estate section of the Sunday paper, we're all required to run a minimum of two ads. If we don't run them,

we get charged for them anyway. But still, all of that does not pay for the page. The company pays part of it.

Most of the respondents stated that they felt that their brokers were justified in retaining a portion of the commission. I expected to find some resentment of the policy, since as independent contractors, it seemed reasonable that salespeople should not have to share their commissions with anyone else. However, such resentment was never expressed to me, and I did probe for such reactions. On the contrary, Tonia Marks's response was typical:

> For me [the broker's share of the commission] is worth it, because I don't want the hassle of being responsible for everything. Even though I am an independent contractor, I still feel like it's his [owner/broker's] business. And this company has a good reputation in the community that it has had for years and years, and I feel like because of that I get a lot of business. I think reputation of the company is important.

Tonia felt that the trade-off was worthwhile. In exchange for a percentage of her commission on each sale, her broker had ultimate responsibility for managing the company. In addition, she benefited from the company's name and reputation. These intangible features were as important as the office space, office equipment, and advertising that the broker/manager provided.

Regardless of the broker's contributions, agents must pay their own social security taxes and arrange for their own health insurance and retirement, as does anyone who is self-employed. Other expenses include advertising, gasoline and all car expenses, monthly fees for the Multiple Listing Service (MLS) and dues to realtors' associations. Sandra Barnes describes many of these expenses in the following account:

> I pay for advertising, all my car expenses. It's funny, we have the magnets on our car doors that say [company name] and people will think that we're provided a company car. What a joke! When we go on vacation, first thing my husband does is take them off. But the biggest expense is the advertising. It can cost forty or fifty dollars for an ad in the Sunday paper. The company provides us with our FOR SALE signs and our lead-in directional signs. We provide the riders with our name and phone number and any other riders that you want to put on the sign, which I do a lot. Especially in these old houses I might have a rider that says "Renovated/Air Conditioned" and I'll put it on top of the sign. Just another little marketing tool. [I pay for] any marketing expenses, any kind of brochure that we might want

to do or any promotional gimmick—refrigerator magnets, anything like that. Postage, legal pads, everything.

This is a fairly typical arrangement, although some companies pay for stationery, or copying, or other office-related expenses. Gasoline and car upkeep expenses are substantial, since agents spend a great deal of time on the road. Realtors usually drive as large a car as they can afford, in part because they often drive clients around to see houses. A large car makes it easier to haul their FOR SALE signs and other equipment. Several mentioned also that they believed it was important to drive a "nice" car—an expensive model—to convey an image of themselves as successful business people. Their clothing budgets were high for the same reason (see below for a discussion of the presentation of self).

In summary, the process by which realtors are compensated is neither as simple nor straightforward as I had believed. Not only do they not receive the entire commission that is included in the cost of a house, they have hefty expenses that come out of their own pockets. Many of these expenses are connected with the realtor's primary focus, attracting customers who will buy houses.

Independent contractors who work under a larger umbrella organization may also be compensated in other ways. In Mary Kay Cosmetics, for example, "consultants" buy products from the company and then sell them to customers at a fixed price. The "commission" equals the difference between the two prices. Independent contractors who are selling only their expertise—for example engineers hired as consultants—would charge a flat fee or an hourly rate.

Finally, the institution of commission sales may become a thing of the past if a new concept gains acceptance, that of fees for service. Proposed by nationally known real estate broker and speaker Julie Garton-Good in her new book, *Real Estate a la Carte,* fees for service would be fixed rates for discrete parts of the realtor's usual package of services. Home buyers or sellers would contract with a realtor to write and negotiate a contract or list a house on the Multiple Listing Service.[9] Garton-Good's argument is that both buyers and sellers are tired of paying a commission and can see parts of the process where they do not need a realtor. Hence, they try to sell their house or find a new house on their own, without the help of any realtors. They usually discover some areas of the process about which they are not sufficiently knowledgeable. The fee-for-service option would allow them to obtain professional help when they need it and not pay a commission for the services they do not need.

Whether the idea of paying fixed prices for various services of a realtor will catch on or not remains to be seen. The industry is divided over the prospect, with many opponents arguing that full representation by a realtor is essential for the protection of buyers and sellers. Even if the option becomes widely available, it is too early to estimate how it will affect commission-based sales and realtors' incomes.

## Sales Volume

I was surprised by the number of houses that most of my respondents had sold in the year prior to our interviews. The volume ranged from twelve to seventy houses in the previous calendar year, with a median volume of twenty-six houses. Sixteen of the women sold between twenty and thirty houses in the previous year. At the two extremes, the two women who sold twelve houses each said that they were selling at the upper price range, i.e., houses costing three hundred fifty thousand dollars or more, while the three who sold over fifty houses each were selling at least some that were in the fifty to sixty thousand dollar range.[10] One of the highest volume respondents was the site agent for two new home sites, but the other two were selling all types of listings. None felt that the previous year had been unusually productive; although three of those in the lower volume (under twenty homes) said that it had been an unusually bad year and that they usually sold more. For example, Elizabeth Rivers had closed twenty-eight sales the previous year and saw that as a low number.[11]

> Last year was a bad year. I think it was because I did so much new construction, and new homes were down some. On the average I usually do thirty-five to forty [closings], and really you should be able to do more than that. This motivational class I just went to, the man thinks you ought to be able to do three or four listings a week. But I would have to have my own private secretary. I mean, there's so much paperwork involved with every transaction.

Elizabeth's statement reveals a contradiction that is common among realtors. On one hand, she indicates that her sales volume was lower than usual because of unspecified market conditions—"new homes were down." There was nothing she could do about it, she was a victim of circumstances. On the other hand, she mentions a motivational class in which the speaker set a volume goal that everyone "ought" to be able to reach (of course, listings and sales are not necessarily connected, although her statement links them.) Here, she seems to believe that her low sales were her fault—she was lazy or not motivated enough.

Respondents expressed this dual definition of the situation repeatedly. The following exchange with Beth Tripp was typical:

> BT: There is an unlimited income potential.
> Q: Do you really believe that the income potential is unlimited?
> BT: Oh, definitely.
> Q: It's limited by the economy, isn't it?
> BT: No. It's unlimited. If I decided today that I was willing to make some changes in my lifestyle with my children, my husband, and house, you know, if those things didn't matter so much. I would have to make a personality change, but I could make one hundred twenty thousand dollars this year, I think, without doing too much different than I'm doing now, just spending more time at it.

Later in her interview, however, Beth Tripp explained that her sales were down that year because "It's a funny market right now." She said she was "down in the mouth" because of slower sales than the previous year. Her response, like Elizabeth Rivers's, alludes to market conditions and personal motivation (it also introduces the question of family obligations and how they affect sales performance, which is discussed in chapter 4.)

From the outside, it is perhaps easier to see this contradiction than it is from the perspective of the realtors themselves. It seemed obvious to me that sales success was determined by objective market conditions as well as subjective characteristics of the individual salespeople. No matter how "motivated" one is, if people are not looking for houses because the economy is slow or interest rates are high, one will sell fewer houses than in the reverse conditions.

The belief that all one needs to succeed is to work hard is endemic to sales work (and of course to the typical American attitude of individualism). It is probably an essential ingredient of the sales person's psyche—to continue going out knocking on doors and pitching a product, one has to believe that the effort will result in success. Robin Leidner describes the qualities of successful sales people: determination, self-motivation, and persistence.[17] These characteristics conform to a conviction that the potential is unlimited if one works hard enough. The faith in hard work is reinforced also by the motivational classes that realtors attend and by speakers at sales meetings and professional conferences. Elaine James explained the importance of motivation:

> For instance, I just took a class this week that cost me sixty-five dollars. You kind of have to pick and choose those. You want to pick the ones that are going to give you the best shot in the arm. They are not required, but let me tell you, in this business, if you are not self-motivated, don't even get into it. I'm not saying that I always am. I have times when I just don't want to think about real estate. But basically, you have to be that kind of person.

Elaine states that the realtor has to be *self*-motivated, but she relies on periodic classes to keep her motivated. Nevertheless, she brings up the important point that in sales work by independent contractors, it is essential to continue going out and making contact with potential customers. Otherwise, the job yields no income.

## Attracting Customers

Residential sales agents use a stock of tried and true measures for attracting new clients and customers,[13] as well as constantly developing new strategies. One of the standard strategies is called "farming." This consists of selecting a particular geographic area—several square blocks, or a distinct neighborhood, or a housing development—and concentrating one's energies in that area. The realtor comes to know what's for sale in that area, the price range, who are the builders, where the schools, shopping and other area services are. S/he focuses on meeting the residents and maintaining a visible presence there. For example, a realtor who is farming a neighborhood might visit all of the homes and leave her business card as well as some sort of token—a cookbook, a refrigerator magnet, a telephone address book—with her name and company logo. She might publish a neighborhood newsletter or send seasonal homeowners' tips to the residents. Elaine James described the farming process as follows:

> I picked an area that was a price range at that time from about fifty-five to ninety thousand [dollars]. Single family. It appealed to me because they were little colonials, everybody's yard was neat. It was just a well-maintained area, a good location. So what you do is, you get out and knock on doors. The initial contact is through a letter. There is a whole procedure that you follow. I had a farming book that tells you exactly what to do. The first step is just to write a letter explaining who you are and that you are going to be specializing in that area, and that you will know everything that's sold, and what it sells for. It just makes a seller feel comfortable that somebody's really keeping up with everything that's going on in that particular area.

Q: How would you know someone else wasn't farming it?
EJ: Oh, you don't! But there's nobody to say that you can't do it anyway. It's a big area and there are about three hundred houses in it, so I figured even if there were somebody else farming it, they couldn't do it all. So I didn't let that deter me.
  And then after the letter, you take something, like a little key chain—I took these rubberized things that help you get tops off—and there's always the company logo. And then after you do that you write a thank you note, if you were able to make contact with a person, if they were at home. You know, you just chit chat with them. People are usually very nice and pleasant if you are, and you just say "I want to take a few minutes of your time and did you receive my letter?" You know most of them just trashed it, and you kind of laugh about it and say "I'm here to introduce myself." I've had people invite me in and show me their house that day. That doesn't mean they're going to list it.
Q: They're trying to figure out what it would sell for?
EJ: Sure! So maybe they're taking a little bit of advantage of you, but you're aware of that, they're aware of that. Then you follow up once every six weeks to two months with a newsletter that kind of updates what's going on, like in the mortgage world. And I'd always include a few tips, like in the spring about planting. Or if it was fall, ways to winterize your home. There are so many things like that that realtors are sent and you can type them up and run them off, and either mail them out or put them in a mailbox or inside the door. I took cookies at Valentine's Day. It's a lot of work.
Q: Did you find it worthwhile?
EJ: I certainly got listings. I started it in October, and I got my first listing in February. It is a wonderful technique for a new agent.

As another form of farming, an agent might canvas the homeowners in an area by telephone. The telephone method would not be as effective as the personal visit, but it might serve to keep the agent's name in the minds of potential sellers.

Other listing procurement techniques include contacting people who are trying to sell their own homes (realtors refer to these as "FIZBOs"—For Sale By Owner) and trying to entice them to list with an agent. Agents solicit listings by advertising her/his selling record, and networking at all kinds of social events—churches, schools, sports facilities, and so on. Deborah Engels, a very successful realtor when I first interviewed her, who has continued to do well, appearing regularly on her company's list of top sellers, tried to describe her procedures for procuring clients:

Well, I don't even know how I do that [get listings] anymore. Some of them are referrals—people tell other people to call me. I send out a newsletter to an area that I call my farm. It's a neighborhood where I used to live, and I've sold a lot of houses there. I do that every month. I order material about homeowner's issues—repairs, winterizing, things like that—from a company [to make up the content of the newsletter] and I include news about the neighborhood. And I've got the names of all the homeowners in the area, which is two hundred fifty homes, on labels. And word of mouth, I guess. People call me. People give my name to somebody else. The other day a customer called me after seeing my picture in the Sunday newspaper—that's a plus for getting your picture in the paper, and our company does that every Sunday. A lot of companies never have the pictures in the paper.

In addition to the newspaper, realtors advertise in industry publications, on the Internet, and on television. There are cable channels devoted entirely to showing pictures and listing prices and features of houses for sale. Also, agents contact sellers whose listing contract with another agent has expired. The point is to be highly visible so that when people decide to sell their home, they will think of that particular agent with whom to list it.

Techniques for attracting buyers for a listing involve advertising in newspapers, on the Internet, in real estate magazines and other trade publications, the MLS, and displaying house signs.

Another popular technique is hosting open houses for prospective buyers and for agents. This latter includes "caravanning," in which several agents from a firm visit sale houses together, often on a particular day each week. For example, several companies organized caravans on Tuesdays, when most of the realtors associated with the participating companies would make the rounds of houses new to the market. This might take several hours but it accomplished the task of increasing awareness of inventory. Realtors' open houses were often held on weekdays and incorporated into the caravans. The listing agent might even serve lunch at the open houses to entice more agents to see the house. Cara Lange used this tactic frequently:

We gave two luncheons last week for agents. What we like to do, and I think it is very successful, is when we have a listing, invite as many real estate agents as we know. Probably you have about one hundred fifty [agents] on a list. You have to print up the cards, mail them out, follow up with phone calls, and then prepare the house and prepare the food. But it works. The agents come through the house. They've gotta eat lunch somewhere and they'll just stop by. This particular one we did last week was really fun. We did lunch at one house and dessert at the other.

I really enjoy doing this. I meet some of the other agents. They like to come because it gives them a chance, when they're really busy they'll say, "Gee, I've been meaning to stop by or call about this house." I personally feel a little badly if people are living in a house to call them for just myself to go through it. But if you can go through it [before taking prospective clients to see it] you can generate more in your mind to tell them about it. I'm not sure I'd do it [the luncheon] at every listing, but I have when I had an unusual house and was trying to get a few more agents to come through it.

Cara's explanation of the luncheons for agents reveals another aspect of the realtor's work—getting other agents interested in a house so that they will show it to their clients. Note, however, that Cara's listings tend to be in the upper-price ranges, where the realtor would recover such an expense with the commission earned (and would be deductible as a business expense).

Salespeople also work to attract customers who are looking for a house to buy and need an agent to help them find it. Agents often acquire clients through referrals, both from other clients and from out-of-town referral services hired by individuals who are relocating to the area or by employers who are transferring employees into the area. In these cases, agents often spend a whole day or more driving the out-of-towners around, perhaps buying them lunch or dinner, and showing them a large number of houses in the amount of time they have in town to locate housing. The following account is from Pamela Rice, who works with a lot of out-of-town referrals:

You really spend concentrated amounts of time when you have an out-of-town buyer. They want to see everything. I might spend a week with an out-of-towner. We might spend two or three days looking, and then we'd do the loan, and then if it's a new house, they have to pick things out for it. So in that week, we'd sort of tie it all up. And the follow-up after that, making sure that the loan is okay, that the attorney has what they need, those incidental type things that take time and you have to do, running papers back and forth and so on, because they aren't here to do it or they don't know the area.

In other types of independent contracting, the process of attracting customers would be different, depending on whether the contractor is soliciting individuals or companies, for a commission or a fee. For example, a mechanical engineer might contract with a large corporation to maintain their refrigeration equipment, for a monthly salary during a specified period of time. The engineer would not be "farming" or advertising his/her services, but contacting companies who advertised an opening in his/her field of expertise.

In real estate sales, the techniques for attracting customers vary with the individual preferences of the realtor. The following section describes some of the variations among realtors in terms of the types of customers and/or houses they prefer.

## Establishing a Niche in the Market

Unlike other kinds of saleswork in which the salesperson simply represents the product s/he is selling, realtors are caught in a complex relationship between home sellers and buyers. Some realtors consider themselves primarily buyers' agents, and concentrate most of their energies on working with buyers. Others consider themselves primarily listing agents, and focus on obtaining listings. The following is Cara Lange's explanation of her preference for working with buyers:

> I spend most of my time finding houses [for prospective buyers]. That is what I prefer to do. There are people that are wonderful with listings. It's not my cup of tea, for one particular reason. Most people get very antsy when they're trying to sell their house, and you can imagine, it's a lot of stress. You don't know when it will be, how much it will be; you don't know what you're going to do. And as they get stressed out, they tend to pick on people, and who is the most likely person? I don't care who they are, they're going to be annoyed at somebody and the realtor is the most likely candidate. That's one of the reasons it's not my favorite thing to do. I do it, but you've gotta really learn how to hang tough.

Another drawback to handling listings is that the agent has to get the house ready for market—in other words, encourage the owners to clean up the house, inside and outside, and make sure that the house is in good shape whenever prospective buyers come to see it. As Pamela Rice indicates in the following remark, this is not always easy:

> If you're listing a house, then you have to do all kinds of stuff about getting the owners to make it look good. And sometimes it's hard to talk to people. It's difficult when you go in and the house is a pigpen, and believe me, I have seen them that are pigpens and you have to say, very tactfully, "You

want top dollar for this, it's got to look, da da da da." And they just can't see it.

On the other hand, agents who prefer to work with listings have equally strongly held reasons for their preference. For example, Beth Tripp explained why she likes doing listings:

> There are lots of reasons [why I prefer to do] listings. You can be more in control than you can if you're working with buyers. With buyers you might go all over town and then they have buyer's remorse, or they walk into an open house and buy without you, whatever. It's hard to have a warm fuzzy relationship with a buyer. Also, if you are doing listings, the work is different. People who don't like paperwork are probably not going to like listings, but I can handle that. Like during open houses I can do my paperwork. Whereas with buyers you get them in the car from nine in the morning until six at night, all day Saturday, all day Sunday, and it's more of a commitment of time and I'm not willing to do that.

Deborah Engels, who also prefers listing, contends that it is sometimes easier than finding houses for buyers:

> Sometimes, in a really good market, all you have to do is stick a sign in a yard. Especially in a hot neighborhood, just stick a sign in a yard, put it in the MLS book, and another agent will come along and sell it. That's the easiest way to make money in the world!

Deborah admits that that kind of situation is not typical:

> This past year has been kind of a slow market, and you have had to have a good balance of buyers and listings. You can't just be a total lister and do extremely well in this market, I don't think. There've been a lot of houses that haven't sold and people get disgusted and they list it with somebody else at a lower price. I've got a house right now, I'm going to have an open house for realtors. You can't just stick a sign in the yard anymore.

As with Deborah Engels, most salespeople engage in both listing houses for sellers and finding houses for buyers, regardless of their preferences. An agent's legal obligation is always to represent the seller's interests, a fact which has caused confusion for buyers who believed that an agent was looking out for their interests first. As Cara Lange explained:

The real estate agent represents the seller, because the seller pays our commission.

Q: So even if you are looking for houses for someone, and you've never met the seller, you still represent the seller?

A: Right, and it's very hard, because the people that you're with are always saying, "Well, what do you think?" or "What would you offer?" And we cannot do that. All I can say is, "This is what it's listed for, these are the comps [houses of comparable value that have sold in the same area] for the area. It's up to you. You have to decide what's the right thing to offer."

This point may be one of the greatest sources of conflict, both between the agent and the prospective buyer and for the agent herself. First, it is logical for buyers to assume that the sales agent who has been showing them houses all over town, calling them when she finds new listings that might fit their preferences, and talking enthusiastically about the houses they view together would be working for them. After confiding their financial status and family needs to her, it would seem that the agent was definitely "on their side." At the same time the agent often gets to know the buyers fairly well and may have never met the sellers, if she is showing another agent's listings, who may very well be from another company. Thus, the agent would possibly identify with the buyers and *want* to help them get the best deal. (See chapter 6 for a discussion of the emotion work involved in selling houses, and how the realtor often finds "helping people" to be a major attraction of the work.)

The real estate industry has tried to alleviate this conflict and protect all the parties involved by developing a disclosure form that realtors must show prospective buyers before beginning to show them houses. However, even with this form, the situation is not completely free of problems. Cara Lange goes on to express her reservations about the form:

> There is a new disclosure form that we're supposed to get them to sign when we're first meeting somebody. Sometimes I have to wait a little longer to do that. I mean, it's a little awkward when you're first meeting somebody to say, "Hi, how are you, what are your real estate needs? Oh, by the way, I want you to know I only represent the seller." It doesn't particularly endear you to a person.

Even after presenting the disclosure form and obtaining the customer's signature, the people who are shopping for a house often ask the kinds of questions that Cara Lange describes previously, and to which the realtor can only respond as she indicated.

In response to this dilemma, the real estate industry conceived of a new legal relationship between realtors and customers. In the 1990s it became legal in some states for agents to contract specifically with a client as a buyers' representative or buyer's agent. This means that the agent represents the interests of the buyer and is under no obligation to a seller. In this newer concept of the buyer's agent, the realtor and the client sign a contract binding the agent to the buyer's interests. The buyer's agent became increasingly popular during the 1990s, and some realtors now focus on that type of work.

I asked each woman how she would represent a buyer if the buyer were interested in a house that she had shown previously and knew from the seller's perspective. The following is a typical answer to my question:

> It is a conflict and you cannot do that. If you came to me and said, "I want to buy a house, and I want you to be my representative," the first thing I would do is show you all the listings of this company, and if you didn't like any of them, then we would enter into the buyer's agent contract. Now what would happen if we'd been looking for several months and a new listing [by her or another agent in her company] came on the market. I couldn't represent you. And you'd have several choices there. You could get another agent, or go to an attorney, or just know that I don't represent you.

In any case, whether as a buyer's agent or in the traditional role of seller's agent, when a salesperson is assisting a client in finding a house, s/he spends a considerable amount of time with the client. The time is important in determining what the client's preferences are as well as, hopefully, insuring the buyer's loyalty throughout the process. Loyalty is a serious concern for many salespeople. Over and over my respondents told me stories of clients in whom they had invested countless hours, who had then found a house on their own and signed a contract without consulting the agent, thus precluding the agent from any commission for her work. This problem is discussed in chapter 6, as one of the negative aspects of the work.

Buyers' agents also "preview" houses for their clients, driving around and touring many houses until they compile a list of those that meet a client's expressed preferences. Previewing homes for prospective buyers means visiting houses for sale by other realtors to determine whether they meet any of the requirements of one's own clients. This activity is time consuming for the realtor, but it saves time for the clients, since the realtor often can eliminate a house based on what she knows about the buyers' preferences. Another incentive for previewing houses is that it gives the realtor an inventory of possible houses for future clients. Previewing is more common for clients in higher price ranges. As Tonia Marks explained:

> I tend to preview real expensive homes for somebody who wants something. But if I'm showing eighty to one hundred thousand dollar houses, I couldn't possibly preview them all. I always tell them "I haven't been through these houses" because it's just too time consuming. I just can't keep up with them all. If you're going to show them ten or twelve houses, you can't preview them, they might be all over the area. If I've got out-of-towners coming in, or land, or something unusual, then I go preview.

One way to facilitate previewing was to attend realtors' open houses, or participate in "caravans," as discussed previously.

Another category of specialization is the site agent, who works at one housing development, either exclusively or primarily—some site agents also work off site part time. Or, if a customer visits the site but doesn't like the homes available there, the site agent might show other listings. Site agents are working with builders selling new houses. They are not the same as a listing agent; in some cases the builder is the listing agent, in others there is a development company coordinating sales for several builders. Site agents may work for a split of the commission or they might be paid a salary plus a fee for each house they sell. Some of their expenses, such as hosting open houses for other realtors, are paid by the builders. The developers pay for some advertising, although the site agent may find it necessary to buy more advertising for specific houses.

Site agents must be very familiar with new construction, although frequently they are new to real estate sales. Usually, as in Sandra Berry's case (quoted previously), they work at a site for a time while they get established and develop contacts. Few choose to stay in site sales indefinitely, since, depending on the price of the homes, the income-earning opportunities tend to be more limited than in general real estate sales work.

## Class and Race Matters

A house, of course, is usually the most expensive consumer product that an individual buys or sells. The buying process may extend over thirty years in the form of a mortgage. Thus, it is a complex matter to determine how much a customer can afford to spend. One of the earliest tasks in working with new clients is to "qualify" them—to determine what they can afford. (Other early tasks include determining what the clients' preferences are in neighborhood, amenities, and housing features.) The residential real estate market is stratified socioeconomically. Neighborhoods tend to contain houses of similar price, within a wide or narrow range. Predictably, realtors also tend to concentrate on particular price ranges in their inventories of listings and the purchasing power of their clients. Although any agent may occasionally sell a house far above or below that range, s/he typically habituates a niche in the market. Thus, some agents predominately sell houses in the fifty thousand to one hundred thousand dollar range; others sell in the three hundred fifty thousand dollars and higher range; others tend to focus somewhere in between. Where an individual locates her/himself depends on the company, its location, the agent's "sphere of influence" (people with whom s/he comes into regular contact and thus draws referrals), and personal inclination. Jennifer Gibson describes how an agent tends toward a particular price range:

> Your listings tend to plug you into a price range. For example, I'm getting ready to list a house for probably about two hundred fifty thousand dollars, and when I hold it open I will be having people, serious buyers, coming in who are going to know that house is two hundred fifty thousand dollars and they're not going to be paying serious attention to it unless they have that kind of money. And if that house is not for them, part of my job is to say, "I would love to keep my eye open for something for you." We have a reputation of dealing in better houses. That's not to say we don't sell small houses when we get the opportunity.

Some agents are very deliberate about targeting a specific price range. For example, Pamela Rice explained that she had chosen from the beginning of her career in real estate to "work smart." By this she meant focusing on establishing a niche for herself in the higher price range so that she would not have to sell as many houses to make an acceptable income:

> I probably sell an average of fifteen to twenty houses a year. Because I sell in the higher price range, I don't have to sell as many to get the big numbers, whereas a lot of agents are working in the fifty [thousand]s, sixty [thousand]s, one hundred [thousand]s. They might sell sixty houses. But I don't do that . . . I sort of got my little niche in selling the high-priced houses so I don't have to sell as many, and I can make good money and have good numbers.

Agents who select the higher price ranges are comfortable working with wealthier clients, and probably have access to social situations that place them in proximity to prospects who can afford their inventory. Thus, Pamela Rice belonged to a country club and deducted the dues as a business expense because she made so many contacts there.

Finally, realtors may find themselves in a racial "niche." Although most respondents insisted that the real estate market is blind to race or ethnicity, some agents work primarily with white clients, and some with black clients. This is a sensitive issue because of notorious "redlining" in the past. Red-lining meant that residential neighborhoods were marked as white, Black, Hispanic, Asian, and so on, and realtors did not show houses to customers of other races. Today, the realtors' code of ethics states that they will not make any distinctions based on race or ethnicity. The white respondents would not acknowledge any race awareness at all. When asked, they all responded in a similarly flat tone that race was irrelevant to their business. For example Tonia Marks, a white woman, insisted that the real estate field is race blind:

> In real estate we don't look at color.
> Q: I know that is true legally, but I'm just wondering if in actuality "everybody knows" that if you're African American you go to a certain company, or whatever?
> A: No. In real estate everybody sells to everybody else.

However, four of the five African American respondents perceived at least some racism in their experiences as agents. Those four women felt that they were discriminated against by their brokers and by white agents. They said that they didn't get a chance at listing higher priced houses or working with customers looking for that price range. When they did succeed, their efforts were less likely to be recognized by the company. Nadia Barnes, an African American respondent cited this example:

> I would be top agent in the company, but they're trying to come in and put this white woman in as the top agent. They tried to say she sold more real estate than I did last year, but I know she didn't. But they want to put her up front because she's white and they want to be identified as white.[14]

One of the four women who perceived racism in real estate worked in a African American–owned company, and said that almost all of her company's customers were African Americans. The other three women worked in white–owned companies, but said that most of their (the individual agents') customers were African Americans. For the most part, they felt that this arrangement was expedient for themselves and their customers as much as for the company, because they could establish good rapport with their customers and build a good network of referrals. At the same time, they recognized that the fact that they worked predominately with African American customers meant that the industry, as U.S. society as a whole, is much more race-conscious, if not racially segregated, than it acknowledges.

This race-consciousness might be acknowledged more openly in other parts of the country. A recent study by a private fair-housing group found that housing in this metropolitan area was racially segregated, with only one in eight residents living in integrated neighborhoods. The group attributed this pattern to discriminatory practices, including redlining and steering. Responses from the local realtors' board denied discrimination while acknowledging that housing patterns are racial and attributing these patterns to historical arrangements.[15] Race was not a focus of my research, and I do not have enough data for further analysis, but this is an important issue for future research.

Thus, realtors can be differentiated in several ways: by their preferences for listing or finding homes, by the price range of the houses they list and/find, by the race of their clients. In the next section, another factor is beginning to separate realtors—the use of electronic marketing tools.

## Cyberselling

The rapid development of electronic marketing via the Internet is affecting realtors' work in unexpected ways. Perhaps most significantly, anyone with a computer and access to the Internet can look for homes for sale on her/his own, without benefit of a realtor. Previously, only realtors had access to Multiple Listing Service—the MLS "big book" that was published within the industry and updated periodically. It contained descriptions of all the houses listed for sale by Realtors® in a given geographic area. Thus, short of driving around and finding "For Sale" signs, a prospective buyer could not search an entire area without the help of a realtor. Now, however, an individual can log onto several sites that list houses all over the country, and choose houses that are of interest before contacting a realtor. That means the buyer will contact the listing agents for specific homes, and may or may not continue to consult that agent if the first home is not the final choice.

Presently, there are several major Internet sites that list homes for sale nationwide (or even internationally). The largest of these is Realtor.com. Others include HomeSeekers.com, CyberHomes.com, HomeAdvisor.com, and HomeShark.com.[16] All of these sites list homes that are under contract with realtors. But another site, Homebytes.com, started in 1999 and listed homes online that owners tried to sell without a realtor. For this latter service, sellers payed Homebytes a fee to list their home online and in the Multiple Listing Service.[17] The owners of these sites are in fierce competition for listings, and vying for exclusive rights to listings. At the same time, local companies and/or individual realtors are developing their own Web sites and presenting their listings. Newspapers also advertise homes on their Web sites.

The potential uses of the Internet are seemingly endless. Eventually, a home shopper will be able to "tour" houses, inside and outside, via computer. Already, buyers can research mortgage loans, apply, and complete the financing procedure on line. And home shoppers can submit profiles of the type of house, neighborhood, price range, and so on that they want. They receive e-mail messages whenever appropriate houses come on the market. As Cara Lange explained in 1998:

> Everything is on the Internet. I had a client call me about a month ago and he found twelve houses on the Internet. He's coming up from Virginia Beach and I'm going to show him all the houses. Of course, I had to go into the computer and pull up what he wanted to see. It's a whole different story because we used to have to figure out what they wanted to see. He found out for me, which is even better. Someone from Washington State can pick out a house in Richmond that they want to see. It is really interesting how that can happen. It is so quick and fast. If you put a listing in the computer it is there immediately. I even have a Web page.

Cara felt that the changes resulting from computerized listings were mostly positive, as did the majority of my respondents. All agreed that a realtor without a computer and Internet access would be seriously handicapped in today's market. They see the realtor's role evolving into that of a manager or intermediary between the buyer and the Internet. According to Roger Conley, a vice-president at HomeStore.com, which is the umbrella site for internet real estate sites, in the future, "[The realtor] will be a transaction manager, obstacle sweeper, time saver, and tour guide through the complex process of buying a home."[18]

The National Association of Realtors estimates that ninety percent of agents own or lease a computer, over sixty percent use e-mail and the Internet in connection with their business, and thirty percent have their own Web pages for business use.[19]

Observers wonder whether the long-term effect will be a huge reduction in the number of jobs available for local realtors. At the 1999 NAR convention, a realtor from California predicted that over half of all real estate jobs and firms will disappear by the year 2010, mostly as a result of a reduced need for realtors because of the use of computer technology.[20] Another consequence might be a commission reduction. There is already pressure to lower commissions to four and a half or three and a half percent when buyers do much of the work of finding a house themselves.

Some respondents in 1999 lamented the "old days" of personal contact, and in general realtors contend that buyers ultimately need the personalized expertise of an in-person agent. Richard Mendenhall, president-elect of the NAR, insisted:

> High-tech will not replace high-touch. People want human contact. They want information personalized. On the Internet, you can't detect a cat smell [inside a home] or notice that an airport is nearby.[21]

I find it significant that the qualities cited as saving the realtor's job—the "high touch" qualities—are those that women realtors cite as their particular strengths as sales agents (see chapter 5). Other technologies that are changing the way realtors do their work include e-mail, cellular phones, scanners, digital cameras, computer software—for comparative market analysis, document preparation, and presentations—and laser printers. In conjunction with realtors, banks and insurance companies can generate and transmit appraisal reports, credit reports, title insurance, and homeowners insurance online. Finally, multimillion dollar homes and other properties are being auctioned on the Internet. The potential uses of these technological innovations are hard to predict and apparently limitless.

## The Realtor's Presentation of Self

Real estate and other forms of interactive service work often require workers to manipulate their identities in self-conscious ways, using their appearance, personality, and emotions as well as physical and intellectual capacities to enhance customers' receptivity to services.[22] Erving Goffman called this process, which we all do to some extent in meeting other people, the "presentation of self."[23]

Realtors believe that it is important to appear professional and successful, which means that they dress carefully and drive cars that convey an appropriate message about their status. They present themselves as competent, enthusiastic about their work and the specific houses they are showing, and interested in the needs and preferences of their clients. Those are characteristics of the self-presentation that all realtors can adopt. In addition, women realtors say that they make an extra effort to display their knowledge of the technical specifications of houses—construction materials, energy efficiency, and the like—as reassurance to customers that they know "as much as a man" about such matters. These would be examples of compensating for possible negative reactions to gender. But more importantly, they present their knowledge of family needs and decorating possibilities as assets that they possess as women. If real estate saleswomen invoke gender attributes as significant to their job performance, then it is probable that the source of these assumptions resides in themselves rather than in their employers, and is the result of cultural expectations.

In explaining their success in a job, workers frequently cite aspects of the work that they define as gender related. For example, in the case of male insurance agents, a sense of independence and a belief that agents could earn as much money as they were worth were important job attributes in affirming the agents' masculinity. Those same attributes are important to realtors in defining their work identities, but apparently are not seen by realtors as masculine, since women realtors experience the same imperative to success. Instead, these attributes may be perceived as gender-neutral, while other characteristics are emphasized selectively by women and men realtors. Chapter 5 discusses the ways that women realtors enact gender in their work. Here it is important merely to note that the nature of the work involves a presentation of self that the women perceive as attached to their gender.

This, then, is the experience of being a real estate agent. As independent contractors, realtors are free to determine their own work schedules, which is one of the attractions of this type of work. The next chapter looks at how the women in this study arranged their work.

## Notes

1. Robin Leidner, *Fast Food, Fast Talk: Service Work and the Routinization of Everyday Life* (Berkeley: University of California Press, 1993), 26.

2. National Association of Realtors, "The Data Bank," NAR *Membership Survey 1999,* http://nar.REALTOR.com/research/papers/member//text.htm (January 11, 2000).

3. Richmond Association of Realtors, "Study Shows What Top Producers Look for When Selecting a Firm," *The Richmond Association of Realtors* (December 1996), 9

4. National Association of Realtors, "The Data Bank."

5. Maureen Connelly and Patricia Rhoton, "Women in Direct Sales: a Comparison of Mary Kay and Amway Sales Workers," in *The Worth of Women's Work: A Qualitative Synthesis,* eds. Anne Statham, Eleanor M. Miller, and Hans O. Mauksch (Albany: State University of New York Press, 1988), 245-264.

6. Barbara J. Thomas and Barbara F. Reskin, "A Woman's Place is Selling Homes: Occupational Change and the Feminization of Real Estate Sales," in *Job Queues, Gender Queues: Explaining Women's Inroads into Male Occupations,* eds. Barbara F. Reskin and Patricia A. Roos (Philadelphia, Pa.: Temple University Press, 1990), 280-289.

7. *Richmond Times-Dispatch,* August 2, 1998.

8. Errors and omissions insurance would protect the agent in the event that s/he were sued by a buyer for not revealing any flaws in the property or liens against it.

9. William Ciucci, "A la Carte ... " *Richmond Times-Dispatch* (June 10, 2001), K-1.A.

10. These are 1990 housing prices. The housing market has appreciated significantly since then.

11. Respondents explained that a sale was not completed until it had closed, and thus they might have had more contracts pending at the end of the year, but their sales volume was based only on completed closings.

12. Robin Leidner, "Serving Hamburgers and Selling Insurance: Gender, Work, and Identity in Interactive Service Jobs," *Gender & Society,* 5, no. 2 (June 1990), 154-177.

13. Respondents used these two terms—customer and client—in contradictory ways. Some used them interchangeably; others specified that customer meant someone looking for a house while client referred to someone selling a house; others used the terms in the opposite way. Still others added the term "prospects" to refer to people who were looking for a house (see J. D. House, *Contemporary Entrepreneurs: The Sociology of Residential Real Estate Agents* [Westport, Conn.: Greenwood Press, 1977], 42, for a similar discussion of these terms). Because of the confusion, I have opted to use the terms interchangeably. Thus, clients, customers, and prospects all refer to people engaged in buying or selling a home through a real estate agent.

14. A realtor who read an early draft of this chapter took issue with this claim, asserting that the total sales volume is a matter of record and a company

would not be able to falsely promote one agent as having higher sales than another.

15. Gordon Hickey and David Ress, "Study Cites Prejudice in Housing," *Richmond Times-Dispatch* (January 12, 1997), A-1.

16. *Richmond Times-Dispatch*, January 9, 2000, L1-3.

17. Homebytes went out of business in the spring of 2001, after losing millions for venture capital investors. Industry analysts believe that the site was poorly organized but that the concept will emerge again.

18. *Richmond Times-Dispatch*, January 9, 2000, L1-3.

19. National Association of Realtors, "The Data Bank," 1999.

20. *Richmond Times Dispatch*, January 9, 2000, L1-3.

21. *Richmond Times-Dispatch,* January 9, 2000, Insert in original.

22. Robin Leidner, "Serving Hamburgers and Selling Insurance," 1991.

23. Erving Goffman, *The Presentation of Self in Everyday Life* (New York, Doubleday Anchor Books, 1959). See also Robin Leidner, "Serving Hamburgers," 1991, for a discussion of how interactive service workers must manipulate their self presentations. While such presentations are perhaps inevitable, they can create stress when they are not congruent with one's true feelings. The costs of such work are described in chapter 6.

# Chapter Three

# Arranging the Workday

The media provide mounting evidence of "time poverty," overwork, and a squeeze on time . . . Competitive forces operate on the self-employed as well. This group . . . clocks in some of the country's longest hours . . . Ominously low survival rates for the self-employed make self-exploitation virtually inevitable.
—**Juliet B. Schor**, *The Overworked American*[1]

I get up around seven-thirty, take my shower, get dressed and leave the house between nine and nine-thirty. I might have an appointment where I'm either going to talk to somebody about listing their house, or show property, or I'll come here to the office to do paperwork. Whatever I'm going to do. I don't know from one day to the next. It's great! Then I always take about half an hour for lunch, then keep on doing whatever I do in the afternoon. Nights, it varies. It can be one night or three or four nights a week.
—**Lana Kight**, six years' experience selling real estate.

The daily structure of residential sales work is typical of many entrepreneurial jobs where workers are free of time clocks and other forms of managerial control. Realtors have to decide how to arrange their workdays since, as independent contractors, they are subject only to themselves for reporting to work. The flexibility of determining their own schedules is one of the primary features that attract people to residential sales work, as will be discussed in chapter 6. At the same time, realtors are responsible for disciplining themselves to work steadily and put in enough hours to earn sufficient income, since all of their income depends on their sales commissions. In the truest sense of the old adage, if they don't work (regularly and diligently), they don't eat. Like Juliet Schor's "overworked American," they are often driven to work longer and harder than if they had jobs with regular nine-to-five hours.

This chapter examines how the women realtors scheduled their work on a daily and a weekly basis to accommodate the many demands of the job while also accomplishing the other tasks of living. To begin to get an understanding of the women's actual workdays, I asked them how many hours they worked per week, on the average. Most of them had some difficulty answering this question, and all explained that the number of hours varied from week to week, depending on the pace of the market and their own particular client load. They had to estimate the number of hours they worked, and the results are therefore susceptible to individual differences in perception.

A further complication in estimating hours was the fact that the work varies according to the weather in general and the seasons of the year in particular. On a daily basis, the work fluctuates by rain, snow, and other inclement weather that make customers less willing to get out and visit houses. But this factor mostly affects the attendance at open houses and the number of drive-by clients who see a "For Sale" sign and decide on the spur of the moment to call the realtor listed and arrange to view the house. For the most part, realtors can work around bad days, catching up on paperwork and phone calls, for example.

It is the seasonal weather cycles that are most significant in shaping work schedules. Specifically, summer and winter, when temperatures reach extremes of heat or cold often accompanied by high humidity or the inclemency of rain or snow, are slower sales times. On the other hand, spring and fall are usually busy times, when the weather is most conducive to customers getting out and looking for new homes. My interviews took place in the winter and very early spring, before the seasonal upswing started. Several of my respondents mentioned that their hours would increase after daylight savings time started, and slacken again when the weather got extremely hot.

In addition to this seasonal cycle of working hours, there are slow and busy periods according to market conditions. When the economy is expanding and interest rates are low, the housing market accelerates and realtors work long hours. Conversely, when the economy slows, fewer people shop for housing. Both the original and the follow-up interviews for this study occurred during strong economic periods when sales in the housing market were brisk. This factor probably offset some of the effects of it being the slower season. The net effect of these two factors—the slower season and the brisk market—was that the women claimed that their estimates were fairly typical of their yearly averages. With the caveats discussed above in mind, the most frequent response to the question of the number of hours worked was over forty hours a week, with some attempts to specify this ranging up to eighty hours. For example, Sandra Berry calculated her work time as follows:

> I don't know. OK, a normal workweek would be forty, plus I try and only work one day on the weekend. Sometimes I only have one or two showings on a weekend, sometimes I work all day. Sometimes I work both days . . . so say eight hours a weekend, and then another eight hours of nights. Let's say sixty hours a week.

Sandra's answer was characteristic of my respondents in the number of hours she calculated that she worked and in her apparent confusion about those hours. Later in her interview, when she described her typical daily schedule, it was obvious to me that she was working at least sixty hours in a "normal" workweek (see next section). Like Sandra, the majority of respondents started by saying that they did not know how many hours they worked a week but then, using a forty hour work week as their base answer, usually arrived at a number around sixty hours and surprised themselves by this discovery. It became evident that the work has a tendency to expand beyond the women's initial expectations, and they had not realized this fact. Once they recognized it, they tried to make sense of this expansion.

Another respondent, Patrice Jefferson, started at an even lower estimate, "I would say about thirty [hours a week]." When I asked her if that was because she was well organized she laughed and replied, "Not at all." After I probed further, it became clear that she had only been considering the hours doing paperwork:

> It's really because most of my time is spent working with customers. I do very little paperwork.
> Q: But if you counted all the time you are with customers, on the phone, and so on?
> PJ: Oh, everything? That's a thought. I should sit down and actually count. I'm probably working myself to death [laughs]! Like yesterday I worked from nine [a.m.] until after eight [p.m.], but I was on the phone for like an

hour after I got home. Most of my appointments are in the evening, so I might go home and cook dinner, or I might go out and eat. And if I walk around the mall, I can talk to a prospect or I'll see someone I know. I usually give out at least five of my business cards a day. And I work all day Saturdays. Let's put it like this, I don't know how many hours I work!

Based on this description, Patrice's weekly workload is closer to sixty hours than thirty. It was interesting to me that her initial response counted only paperwork as "work." I wondered if it was because that was the part of the job that she enjoyed least, and thus it felt like work in contrast to her enjoyment of meeting people and showing houses. It introduces an intriguing boundary issue. Do we define work as only those activities that we do not enjoy? Certainly it is common to hear people say that an activity did not seem like work because they were having so much fun. I shall consider this question further in chapter 6.

Once they had thought about it carefully, the women estimated that they worked more than they would have in a traditional eight-hours-a-day, five-days-a-week job. They were spending a lot of time on the phone (or, by 1998, on the Internet), doing paperwork and meeting customers. The work tended to expand to fill most of their time, although they were often able to take "personal time" off and on throughout the day. Evenings and weekends of work more than made up for those personal times. But because they enjoyed the work and felt that they controlled the amount of time they hadn't realized how much they were working.

Heather Sloan was unusual in achieving a shorter workweek, and even she admitted that it would take her a few more years to reach her goal:

> I'm . . . very organized, and I felt that if I could be really, really organized I could make a very good salary working maybe twenty to twenty-five hours a week . . . And also I didn't want anybody telling me I had to be somewhere, do something. If I make a commitment to something, I do it on my time when I want to . . . I'm always there by phone, and my appointments are always scheduled.
>
> I'm getting close to [twenty to twenty-five hours a week] some weeks. Some weeks though, it's quite a bit more . . . I was at everybody's beck and call the first two and a half years. I was running crazy from one side of town to another.

Heather had found that accomplishing control over her work hours was difficult and could only be done by making that control a priority:

I really believe that there are too many realtors who run around at the beck and call of their sellers and buyers. I pretty much work that I'm available at this time, this time, and this time. If they take off work to meet their doctor or lawyer, they can do it to meet their realtor. And I may lose some business for it, but I think I get a lot of respect from people.

Heather was more aware than many of the respondents of the need to be conscious of the hours worked, and she was determined to control her schedule so that her hours were shorter, her work compacted into a smaller framework. However, as Heather described her actual schedule (see the next section), it was clear that she, like Sandra Berry, was working regularly many more hours than she had estimated.

In comparing the women's responses in the initial interviews, it seemed that the number of hours required tended to decline with years of experience. Of those women who had been selling for at least four years in 1990, fifty percent said that they worked fewer than forty hours a week. Whether they actually did or not is less certain, since their detailed descriptions tended to reveal many more hours than they had been counting. For example, Fiona Miller said that she had switched companies and was now working "about forty hours a week" (she had previously handled the relocation department, a nine-to-five job, and her own sales which meant that she had worked far more in that position). But Fiona still spent every day, including Saturdays and Sundays, and most evenings working, so her hours added up to far more than forty. Those with four or more years of experience were more likely to confine more of their work to weekdays, with a maximum of one or two nights and one day a weekend of work.

By contrast, all of the women who had been selling for less than four years believed that they worked more than forty hours a week. Those women who had started selling recently were likely to work longer hours, and to work more nights and weekends.

In the follow-up interviews in 1998, however, the pattern of working fewer hours with seniority did not hold true. At that time, eighty-five percent of the women reported that they worked a minimum of forty hours a week, and said that most weeks they worked longer than that, averaging forty-five to fifty hours a week. Again, their descriptions of their workdays indicated that they might have underestimated the amount of time they were working. Fiona Miller, still with the same company as in 1990, now estimated that she worked sixty to sixty-five hours a week. Patrice Jefferson had changed companies and answered in 1998:

> I'd say about forty-five hours a week, plus weekends. I work every weekend—showings, phone calls, paperwork. I cut out a little early on Sundays.

Perhaps the consistently long hours in 1998 can be explained by the conditions of the housing market, which were at an even higher point than they had been in 1990, after rebounding dramatically from a low period in the mid-1990s. Only one woman, Ginger Allen, who previously had estimated her work weeks as sixty to seventy hours, had reduced her hours to about twenty in 1998, but she had reduced her sales work to very limited hours because of additional family obligations:

> I don't sell as much as I used to. I am expecting my eighth child and we homeschool our children and so that pretty much takes priority. There is no way I can work full-time or part-time so what I do now is just take on one or two clients compared to back when we weren't involved in homeschool and I was selling like fifty houses a year.[2]

With this exception, the women had not reduced their work hours below a full-time work week as they became more experienced realtors. They were, however, less likely than they had been in 1990 to work seventy or more hours a week. For example, Drew McCain said in 1990 that her "average has been all day and all night, seven days a week." In 1998, with twelve years of experience, she said,

> Since I am trying to get away from the stress I try to limit my hours . . . so I'd guess about forty hours for me, a little more if I work weekends. But there is tremendous fluctuation in hours.

With the exception of Ginger Allen, noted above (who was exceptional anyway, in having seven children and being pregnant with an eighth child), the number or ages of their children did not affect the number of hours per week that the women worked. I found this surprising; I had expected that domestic responsibilities would limit the women's time commitment to their paid work. However, my sampling method limited the variations among the respondents—I focused on women with children twelve years of age or younger, so I cannot compare the hours that they worked with those of child-free women. Some of the women did say that their family responsibilities had limited their work performance, and they profiled the "ideal realtor" as a divorced woman without children at home (see Beth Tripp's comment about the unlimited income potential of the field at the end of chapter 2. This issue is also discussed in chapter 4.)

Launching a career in real estate sales requires working long hours in order to earn enough money to be able to stay in the business. The women had to work as long as the job demanded to establish themselves in the field, regardless of whether or not they had children. It is probable that any sort of independent contracting sales work requires long hours. The women who had young children were able to work long hours only by making adaptations in their family-related work, as will be discussed in chapter 4. They had to have help with their domestic responsibilities. They either hired that help, in the form of babysitters or day-care facilities, or they had family support.

## Scheduling Work

A typical workday would be to get here around nine to nine-thirty [A.M.] and do paperwork and make phone calls, make appointments to show houses. It is just a constant thing and then I have to squeeze in time for myself. So I just kind of stay real busy. I schedule a lot. I am really good at time management.
—**Deborah Engels**

While the women felt obligated to work long hours, they felt that they could spread those hours out over the weekdays, evenings, and weekends so that they had blocks of time free for family activities and personal time. As one woman explained, "It's not your time that's flexible; it's your schedule that's flexible." In other words, realtors usually need to work long hours to generate sufficient income, but they can take breaks at many intervals during the day, so long as they return to work at another time.

Generally, the women realtors tried to keep a schedule of regular working hours even though their work demands varied from day to day according to customers' needs and the number of houses they had listed. Most of the respondents started working by eight or nine in the morning on weekdays and continued until at least three or four in the afternoon. This time was filled with paperwork, phone calls, previewing homes for clients, and overseeing various types of inspections. Late afternoons and evenings often involved making more phone calls, showing homes to buyers, writing contracts. Each of these activities required a great deal of time, and was crucial to the process of shepherding a sale from the buyer's initial offer or the seller's listing criteria to the final closing. Kendra Jones described her daily schedule as follows:

Most mornings I'm here between eight-thirty and nine [o'clock]. If I have a contract coming in I might be here at eight [A.M.]. Sometimes I have to run contracts or do paperwork, or meet a termite inspector or an appraiser for a listing, or something like that. And if that's at nine-thirty [A.M.] or sometime like that, I'll just leave from home to do that. Then I'll come in and pull the "hot sheet" (that's new listings that come off the computer every day) and go through it. So I'll go through and list the ones [new listings off the hot sheet] I want to pull off the computer, and then I'll go pull them [the full descriptions]. Then I might call somebody after that, if I thought there was something they might like to see. Or I might be working on a contract. I might show a house during the day. A lot of people can get off from work for an hour or so if something comes up. Also, I'll have appraisals, home inspections on my listings and my sales.

This schedule sounds full but straightforward—working all of the obligatory meetings into the day. However, these assignations frequently did not occur as arranged. Kendra said that she had not anticipated the amount of time spent making arrangements with all of the parties involved:

Sometimes for listings, you have to meet another agent at your listing. Sometimes you're writing notes, letters. You're on the phone a lot. That's the one thing that has shocked me. I feel like I stay on the phone some days for hours. Because you make a call and you've got to wait for somebody. And you have to check on the loans. And that takes time, when you've got five, six, seven in the pocket [houses under contract, awaiting loan approval and so on.]

Elaine James enumerated several other tasks that might make up part of the daily schedule:

Like right now I'm working with an out-of-towner that bought a house, and I've done everything. I mean, because they're not physically here to do it, they took the loan application, but I've met the fence man—this is a brand new house, they want a fence up, I've had to do that. I've met the wallpaper people; I've met a carpenter to have a dog door put in.

This account sounded unusual to me, and I thought perhaps such involvement occurred because the clients were moving from out of town. However, several other respondents described similar processes of high involvement with the buyers, including arranging for house inspections, being physically present for these and for utilities workers, and doing some of the legwork on the loan applications. In short, the realtor's day can involve a wide variety of obligations.

In addition to all of the time required for scheduling appointments with the various participants in each transaction, realtors had to complete paperwork on each step. The house purchasing process involves a great deal of paperwork. Kendra Jones again:

> Paper work is horrendous. You wouldn't think there'd be a lot of paper work, but there is, either for a listing or a sale. We have a packet we fill out for a listing, and we have to write our ads, ad copy and all that. On a sale, you have to fill out an information sheet, and contract, and so on.

Kendra did not have any specific days that she gave herself as nonworking days each week, but many of the respondents did. For example, Vicki Gray made it a practice to take Wednesdays as "personal" days, as an alternative to having Saturdays and Sundays off, and many women had a similar practice, of taking one weekday off from their real estate sales work, as compensation for working on the weekends. However, Vicki was also typical in finding that those "off" days were often interrupted by phone calls or other unscheduled work:

> I've tried from the beginning to make it perfectly clear that Wednesday is my day off. And I would stay home. And I'd stay on the phone all day long. People would say, [making her voice high and accusatory] "Are you enjoying your day off? What are you doing taking a day off in the middle of the week?" If you're going to take a day off, the only thing you can do is get out of town. And even then, you have to call in for messages. You can turn your work over to somebody, but it doesn't go over very well because it's such a people business. If you leave your home with me, you're listing because of me; you're not listing because of the [company] sign in the yard.

Obviously, Vicki's perception of her responsibilities to her clients was different from Heather Sloane's, quoted previously in this chapter, and resulted in much longer workweeks. From my interviews, Vicki was more typical of women realtors, since most worked far longer than the twenty to twenty-five hours a week that Heather envisioned.

Tess White tried to work Monday through Thursday, take off on Friday, and work Saturday and Sunday. The rest of Tess's schedule was much like Kendra Jones's schedule: On weekdays, she ran errands in the mornings—dropping off contracts, picking up materials, meeting housing inspectors. Tess did paperwork and phone work at her office in the afternoons. Also during the day, she spent time previewing homes. In the evenings, she did a lot of work at home by telephone, talking to buyers and sellers. When she was working with local buyers, she would pick them up after they finished work and take them to view houses by appointments that she would have scheduled previously with the owners or the listing agent. If the buyers were visiting from out of town, then she probably would spend most of the day with them, or perhaps with the wife while the husband was busy with business meetings. Tess said that on weeknights, "It's not unusual for me to get home at eleven or eleven thirty." On Saturdays she usually worked about half a day, and Sunday afternoons she often hosted an open house from noon to five o'clock.

This schedule adds up to fifty or more working hours a week. While I have included here only the activities that relate to her real estate work, Tess and most of the other respondents actually intersperse their descriptions of work-related and family-related activities. The description above represents only a "skeleton" of Tess's week—the real-estate part. Her household labor provides the flesh that fills out her weeks. The complexity of the arrangements for both spheres will become apparent in chapter 4.

The working hours have to be compatible with the needs of prospective clients, which means that most realtors spend at least some evenings and weekends showing homes, making listing presentations, writing contracts, and so on. While a few of the women with several years of experience in real estate sales did not work regularly on the weekends, most realtors do work at least part of most weekends. As Vicki Gray, who had been selling real estate for six years explained:

> Obviously, you're going to work Saturday and Sunday. They're your prime days, just like a restaurant. Do you close a restaurant on Friday night? No, not if you want to stay in business.

By contrast to the majority, a few women had managed to eliminate most weekend and evening work. One of them, Lana Kight, had been selling residential real estate for six years:

> When I first started in this business, I did everything seven days a week. Then I realized you can make money in this business and do a good job Monday through Friday. I'd been to enough seminars, and all this [motivational] stuff to realize that this is how superstars conduct their business. I'm talking about people who do fifteen to twenty million[3] a year. If you could get people to understand, they take off to go their accountant, to go to their doctor, to go to their lawyer, they can take off to go look at houses. And

people will do that. All you have to do is ask. It's amazing.

However, Lana admitted that she still worked one or two nights most weeks:

> It can be one night or three or four nights a week, if that's the only time people can see me and talk to me. If they can do it during the day, I ask them. But I had a week two weeks ago where I was out three nights, negotiating contracts, a counter offer going back and forth, that kind of thing.

In 1990, Lana's company had established a kiosk at a local shopping mall (a strategy that was more common by 1998), and the agents took turns working there. For example, Lana had recently worked a shift at the kiosk from seven to ten o'clock in the evening. She usually worked one shift every six days. Lana considered working at the kiosk a productive use of her time since it served as a "way to get prospects for business." People strolling by the kiosk frequently stopped to "browse," giving the agent on duty a chance to introduce her/himself and determine what their housing interests were.

Finally, all of the women emphasized that, no matter how careful they were to develop and adhere to a schedule, there were always unexpected events that could disrupt that schedule. Patrice Jefferson explained:

> You can sit down the night before and plan out your day, which I like to do. And then you get one phone call the next day while you're putting on your makeup that will throw everything off by two hours. Or you're never going to get it done that way because somebody doesn't show up, or somebody else does. Just one fire after another to put out.

Although these "fires" were disruptive of the daily routine, and made it difficult to plan ahead, the constantly changing activities that made up a typical workday were one of the major attractions of the work, as will be discussed in chapter 6.

## Where to Work

> I don't come into the office much. I'll come in only if I have something specific to do, or it's my office duty day—everybody has office duty days. Other than that, I don't come in much
> —**Allison Foote**

All of the women had developed regular routines for themselves to get their real estate work done efficiently, and each had her own preference about where she worked. Although as one woman said, "If you're in the office, you're not selling real estate," in reality there was a great deal of work that had to be done in an office of some sort. Those who preferred to work more at home disciplined themselves to focus on real estate and exclude household responsibilities for certain intervals. The advantage of being able to do both at once was attractive also, as in the case of Heather Sloane, who was the mother of a nine-year-old boy and a fourteen-month-old girl. She explained that she did paperwork and phone work while her son was in school and her daughter was napping. She took her daughter with her to deliver documents. When she had to present a contract or take care of other business, she took her daughter to a neighbor, who served as a drop-in babysitter. When her children were at home, she found ways to work and be with them at the same time:

> I get my little boy from school at three [o'clock]. . . . He does his homework, and while we're doing that I place calls. I have a portable phone, so I can cook dinner or do whatever while I'm on the phone. I take the phone off the hook usually from six until about eight [o'clock P.M.], my time to have dinner with my family and bathe my children. Usually my children go to bed at seven thirty [P.M.], and from then until nine or ten [P.M.] I'm on the phone or doing whatever.

She frequently hosted open houses and showed houses to clients on weekends, when her husband was at home with the children.

Pamela Rice, who also liked to work at home preferred to do that work when her children, ages nine and twelve, were in school:

> I have an office at the back of my house, and after I get the children to school, I go back there and get my phone calls and things done. I do a lot of that. I might run out and show a house, come back, make phone calls, run down and throw a load of clothes in the washing machine, put the dirty dishes in the dishwasher. That's what I like about working out of my house: I can kind of keep it all together.

Other women did not want to "keep it all together" in this way. They felt that they needed to be in their offices, to be in contact with other agents and to be available to drop-in clients, or because they were too easily distracted by housework at home. For them the times spent on real estate and family work were more distinct, but the intermingling still occurred.

Sandra Berry took her two preschool-age children to a daycare center every weekday while she worked at her office:

> I try to be in the office by nine [A.M.] ... I usually try and wrap up whatever I'm doing during the workday to pick up the kids by five [P.M.]. So we get home, have dinner; my husband's home by quarter of six; I'm out the door, showing [houses], probably until nine thirty, ten [P.M.]. I make a point to, unless it's something pressing, I just try and end everything at ten. So by ten, I'm usually going down to the basement and getting a mess of the clothes and bringing them up, and I'll turn on the T.V. and fold laundry from ten to eleven [o'clock], and then collapse.

Where they worked, whether at home or at their offices, was a matter of personal preference and opportunity. It depended in part on how each woman perceived the relationship between home and work, how rigid or permeable she believed the boundaries should be between the two spheres of her life. In summary, all of the women had developed regular routines to get their real estate work done efficiently. They had also made arrangements to manage their household and family responsibilities. The next chapter describes the relationship of these arrangements to the women's family roles.

## Notes

1. Juliet Shor, *The Overworked American* (New York: Basic Books, 1991), 5, 70.

2. Ginger is so far outside of the norm, of realtors or of working women in general, in having seven children and home-schooling them while she also maintains a busy real estate practice, that I might have excluded her from my sample. But in 1990 she was the mother of "only" three children and her work pattern was typical of the busiest women in my sample.

3. This figure represents the prices of the homes sold, not the commissions earnings for the realtors.

# Part Two

# The Home Is Still Their Domain: Women Work within and outside of Their Family Responsibilities

## Chapter Four

# Homework: Women as Realtors, Wives, and Mothers

> The connection between work and the family is more than understanding the interaction between two separate spheres. . . . Life is lived as an entity, not as separate spheres. Work and parenthood can be combined in a number of different ways. Workplace culture, the conditions set by work and the worker's hierarchic or occupational position largely define the freedom for maneuver in relation to parenthood in the workplace. Even at one workplace many possible ways of integrating work and the family can be found.
> —**Riikka Kivimaki**, "Work and Parenthood"[1]

> I think it's a good profession for women as long as they don't let it become an obsession, if they have a family. If they don't have a family, it can be an obsession! I think you have to try to balance the two.
> —**Kendra Jones**, five years' experience selling real estate.

In the United States today, the majority of women who are in the paid labor force are married, and a high percentage of them have children who are under the age of eighteen years. More specifically, sixty-one percent of married women, seventy-four percent of divorced women, and sixty-eight percent of women with children under eighteen years of age are in the paid labor force.[2] Like the national averages, most of the women in this study were selling real estate full-time and were managing households as wives and mothers. Ninety-seven percent of the women had children; eighty percent had at least one child who was twelve years old or younger in 1990. The remaining twenty percent of the women with children had been selling real estate since their children were younger than twelve, and could remember how they had arranged real estate and family work in those years. Twenty percent of the women with children were divorced or separated from their husbands, and forty percent of these single women had children younger than twelve.

Thus, most of the women whom I interviewed were "balancing" roles as realtors, mothers, and wives in 1990. By 1998, several of these women no longer had young children at home, and the proportion of their time spent on family work and paid work had changed. This chapter examines the ways that the women accomplished their various jobs, and compares those methods in the two time periods—when they had younger children at home and after the children had grown and, in many cases, left home. It provides an example of the ways that women's performance of their paid work is influenced by their family responsibilities. However, in looking back at how the women arranged their schedules and decided whether they preferred to work at home or at the office, it is apparent that there are different ways of negotiating the boundaries between family and work. Work structure and family composition influence the ways that these two factors, paid work and family work, relate to each other.

Finally, a society's gender system shapes the relationship between work and parenthood.[3] In households where husbands and wives share the "breadwinner's" role, both working for pay to provide economic support for the family, women tend to perform more of the household tasks than men perform.[4] Although men are doing more of this work than they did in the past, women are more likely to feel deeply torn between their work and family demands, even in cases where men share the housework. Women, as wives and mothers, feel that the organizational and managerial tasks of deciding what needs to be done and when are their responsibilities.[5] Arlie Hochschild found that when the time it takes to do a paid job, housework, and child care are added together, women work about fifteen hours a week, or an extra month of twenty-four-hour days each year, longer than men.[6] Given this division of labor, women who are involved in both paid and family work are likely to be overburdened, working what amounts to double days, at home and outside of the home. The necessity of coping with such double days may influence the choices women make about the kinds of paid work that they do.

Suggestions for easing the burden of working and caring for families range from redesigning societal definitions of work to individual restructuring of paid or family work. Employer-provided options such as part-time work, job sharing, flexible hours, and family leaves would meet some of the needs of workers with families. On the individual level, workers make permanent or temporary changes in the number of hours they work, their hours of arrival and departure, evening and weekend work, and occasional times off in order to accommodate family responsibilities. This sort of restructuring is related to occupation: flexibility and control over the workday allow individuals to reduce their work hours or otherwise rearrange work for family needs.[7]

Another way to ease the stress of combining paid and unpaid work is to change the division of labor at home, so that men share more equitably in child care and housework. This sort of change requires both structural and ideological considerations. Structurally, fathers' availability is a key factor in determining their participation in child care. Father involvement increases when they and their wives work nonoverlapping hours, indicating that the reason for greater involvement is the fact that only one parent at a time can be with the children. Father involvement is greatest when wives work weekends and/or nights, which would be times when it would be most difficult to find alternative child care.[8]

Regardless of work scheduling, however, assumptions about who should do what affect the household division of labor. The dominant ideology in our society continues to be one that assumes that children and housework are women's responsibilities, not men's or the state's.

For example, children's schools are organized on the assumption that parents, but usually mothers, are available to help with activities. Teachers often rely on "room mothers" to organize holiday parties, chaperone field trips, and assist with classroom projects. School events such as spelling bees and awards ceremonies are usually scheduled during school hours. Parent-teacher conferences have traditionally been scheduled during school hours or immediately after children leave. While fathers also participate in each of these activities, especially as women become increasingly less likely to be full-time stay-at-home mothers, it remains difficult for parents to take time off work to attend to children's needs. And schools have not been financially able to replace their volunteer work force with paid assistants. Hence, planners continue to presume that expenditures of time and effort by mothers will coincide with the needs of schools.[9] As a result of these and other arrangements, women, much more often than men, must find paid work that is compatible with their family obligations.[10]

The assumption that women are primarily responsible for children and housework is so taken for granted that most women and men do not question it, but work out a division of labor based on it.[11] When husbands do participate in household labor, they are said to be "helping," and wives are grateful for any amount of housework and child care that their husbands contribute. Otherwise, women mitigate the burden of housework by employing domestic workers at much lower wages than they themselves earn, or relying on the unpaid assistance of relatives and neighbors.[12]

For women working in residential real estate sales, their work lives are shaped by all of these factors: the nature of the work, the schedules of their spouses, their gender ideologies, and the availability of other household laborers. The structure of this work would seem to make it attractive to women with children at home. The individual realtors' ability to arrange their schedules according to their personal preferences suits the mother's need for adaptability. The work schedules of realtors are often compatible with spousal care for children, at least during the evening and weekend work times and if their spouses work regular schedules of fixed hours.

This chapter analyzes how the women realtors who were mothers and/or wives interwove their paid and unpaid labor, considering the relative flexibility and constraints of both types of work, and the kinds of adaptations that the women made in each sphere. The ways that these women managed household work and sales work provide insights into the conditions of work and family life that contribute to or inhibit the satisfactory accomplishment of activities in each sphere.

## The Expectation of Compatibility

One of the reasons that residential sales work attracts women with children is that they expect to be able to do their sales work during times of the day and week that they do not have to meet household obligations.[13] Work in this field differs from most other occupations that have been open to women, which require employees to be at work for specified hours during the day or night.[14] In a 1986 study, real estate brokers described the ideal salesperson as "a young married woman with a couple of children and a successful husband":

> Because she is young, she will have energy. Because she has children, she will know how to get things done and handle responsibility. Because she has a successful husband, she will be used to having nice things, money, and will be familiar with success.[15]

Consistent with previous findings,[16] the women whom I interviewed said that they had entered real estate sales because they believed they would succeed in the job and in fulfilling family obligations. They needed and/or wanted to work, but they also needed to feel that the job they chose would give them some control over their working hours. In comparing the job with other occupations open to them, the women agreed that it was more flexible than most, at least in not requiring specific hours for work. Tess White, whose two children were in preschool, had worked for the state for several years before going into real estate:

> After I'd had [her older daughter], I began to feel like I didn't want to get up at six [o'clock A.M.], be at work at eight, get off work at five [P.M.], and come home at six. Like the other day, I had to make bunny cakes for the preschool [and] I'm able to take off a half-day and make bunny cakes and take them to school. So I've got that flexibility. When my kids are sick, I can take them to the doctor.

As previously noted, however, it is the scheduling of the work that is flexible; realtors must work long hours to compete successfully in the field. The flexibility of scheduling is counterbalanced by the long hours. The work is never over, since the phone rings day and night. Sandra Berry, who in chapter 3 described folding laundry after working until ten o'clock at night, found that the job can be all-consuming:

> It's not a nine to five job. It's with you all day and all night. It encroaches on your family time too. I mean, I worked all day Saturday, I got home, my husband says, "We're going out for pizza." We all pile in the car. But there were three messages I had to return, so I'm returning these calls in the car going to [the restaurant]. It was frustrating for [her husband] but they were important calls that I had to return and I chose to do it in the car rather than waiting fifteen more minutes at home, or trying to do it when we got home and the kids needed their baths.

As Sandra Berry's account indicates, the work of selling real estate is compatible with family work only to a degree, and only if the burden of family work is shared by someone else. In Sandra's case, her husband had cared for their children on the Saturday that she worked at her real estate job. He had also planned for dinner so that she was not responsible for that domestic task. She could not have worked that day without his or someone else's acceptance of these family responsibilities.

Thus, in spite of the relative compatibility of real estate work and family work, both are too demanding to permit women to do all of both jobs themselves. The ways that the women with families who worked full-time in real estate sales accomplished their various tasks were influenced by the division of labor between themselves and their husbands, and by other types of household help that were available to them.

## Job Sharing at Home

Arlie Hochschild employs the metaphor of a "second shift" in referring to the housework, child care, and household management tasks that must be accomplished before and after one's paid work.[17] Women shared the second shift with their husbands, mothers, other relatives, and/or hired workers, including baby-sitters, day-care providers, and housekeepers, although for the most part they felt responsible for the household and fulfilled its managerial roles themselves.

Husbands were the most significant participants in the household work. A majority (sixty-three percent) of the married women described their husbands as sharing a large portion of housework and/or child-care. Tonia Marks represented the most egalitarian division of labor: "We probably have a seventy/seventy share at home. In other words, we both do everything." She believed that it was essential for husbands to do an equal share of the domestic labor if women are to succeed in combining a real estate career with their family responsibilities:

> I do have, and always have had, the support of my husband. People who know me in this business know [her husband] and they just know how good he's been. I couldn't do this without him. That's what allowed us to [succeed], for everybody to pitch in. Everybody does laundry. My youngest child at four years old knew how to scramble eggs and put them in the microwave. My husband does laundry, and he helps clean. Everybody has to cooperate.[18]

Tonia's account is one of the few that also acknowledges the children's role in the second shift. While she and her husband had worked their schedules so that one was always at home with the children when they were younger, the children had learned how to do many of the household tasks themselves. As they grew older, their tasks became more complex and they were responsible for keeping their own rooms and clothes in order, as well as helping with the rest of the house and lawn work. I did not ask specifically about the children's contributions, so it is not possible to say whether Tonia's household division of labor was common or not. Other parents may have enrolled their children in more or fewer tasks, or relied entirely on their spouses and/or paid helpers.

Another twelve percent of the women said that their husbands did very little housework but shared child care equitably. The remaining twenty-five percent believed that their husbands did little child care or housework. The ages of the children did not affect the reported levels of husbands' involvement in housework and child care. The women with preschool-age children reported the same percentages of high and low husband involvement in household labor as did the women with older children.

The respondents' perceptions of their husbands' share in household labor were different from most of the published research on the household division of labor.[19] Almost two-thirds of the married women believed that their husbands shared more of the household labor than they believed the average husband did.

One explanation of this apparent difference is that the wives' perceptions did not match their husbands' behavior. It is possible that the women were inaccurate in their assessments of their husbands' input, either because they perceived the men as doing more than they actually did or because they wanted me to believe that their husbands were sharing more equally. For example, Heather Sloan (quoted at the beginning of chapter 3) said that her husband did half of the housework and child care. He is absent from her description of her days of interweaving sales work and household labor, however, and she said that he travels during the week, often not getting home until late evening. This sort of discrepancy is often the result of an illusion that reflects ideological shifts: if people believe that a change in the division of labor is desirable, they are more prone to perceive that they have achieved that state of affairs.[20] In a study of the division of labor in marriage, Carolyn Dryden found a similar sort of discrepancy between what her respondents said at different points in their interviews.[21] She attributes this inconsistency to "meaning making" about the marital relationship. Couples construct relational identities according to the values of their society, which in the present include equality between husband and wife. I think this same form of meaning making might have been occurring among my respondents.

On the other hand, it may be that the husbands of the women whom I interviewed really did more housework and child care than husbands in previous studies. Since the data do not provide conclusive evidence one way or the other, I want to explore this second possibility and consider which conditions of work and family life might contribute to husbands sharing more of the household labor. Perhaps the real estate sales work, in combination with other factors, resulted for some of these families in a more egalitarian division of labor.

One factor that may have contributed to husbands sharing more of the household labor was the husbands' occupations and/or work schedules. The husbands who were described as doing a high proportion of household work tended to have jobs that gave them flexible hours or schedules that dovetailed compatibly with their wives' schedules. These husbands included a high school teacher, a clinical psychologist in private practice, a fireman, and several men who were self-employed in sales (including real estate) or small businesses that allowed them to work around their wives' schedules. The wives' work in real estate increased the possibility of scheduling nonoverlapping hours with their husbands. Tonia Marks's husband, who was so cooperative in their "seventy/seventy share," fell into this category as a school teacher:

> We did not ever have the latchkey situation. It worked out that my husband or I was home when they got home. My husband normally gets home at three-thirty [P.M.]. For us, this works well. My husband's got a very steady job. He's been teaching for twenty-odd years. He has a very steady income. He has very steady hours.

For Tonia, then, the steadiness of her husband's schedule, combined with his early arrival home from work in the afternoons, was compatible with her need to work evenings and weekends, and to be more spontaneous in her scheduling.

By contrast, Gillian Greene's husband was a manager of commercial properties and had a very flexible schedule that allowed him to participate fully in domestic labor:

> In his business, he has flexible hours also, so there may be afternoons when he's done at three o'clock. He loves to cook. He laughed last night and said "Plan on my cooking tomorrow night," and I could tell he didn't like what we'd had for dinner, because I had cooked. And that's fine with me, I hate it. So most of the time I don't have to worry about dinner. And he will take [the children] to do fun things, or they might go off and buy the notebook that they need to get. So they really know that Dad is just as capable as mom. Daddy knows how to turn the washing machine on, Daddy knows car pools.

Gillian's husband did not get home at the same time every day, but he usually could come home whenever he needed to, and he shared household work as fully as did Tonia's husband.

In the same way, their husbands' occupations were one explanation for the lack of involvement of the husbands who did little housework or child care. Jennifer Gordon believed that her husband, who had started his consulting business a year earlier, would "help" more if he had the time:

> He works eighty hours a week. There's no way [for him to do household work]. We used to have a setup where he cooked three days a week and I cooked four, but somehow that system fell apart and he quit doing it. He just doesn't have the time now.

It is unclear from her response whether Jennifer's husband quit cooking because of his new business or for some other reasons. Her response implies the former, although she says that "somehow that system fell apart and he quit." At any rate, she does not think he has the time now.

Another possible explanation of high husband involvement in household work was that the wives' relatively high contributions to the economic support of their families gave them more power to demand their husbands' participation in housekeeping and child care chores. In contrast to women in the traditionally female job sector, whose earnings typically are lower than their husbands', the women realtors had acquired a greater share of the provider role. Consequently, they might have been able to extricate themselves more from the housewife role.[22] A few of the women stated or implied this explanation. For example, Laura Howell said that her husband cooperated in the housework and child care because "He loves the checks" that she earns and "He knows that I couldn't do this without him." However, there was no consistent relationship between the husbands' incomes relative to the wives' and their level of involvement in household labor.

Another factor in determining a husband's level of participation in household labor was either spouse's gender ideology. Some of the women who said that their husbands did not do much work at home said that they or their husbands believed that housework and child care were women's work. Tess White's husband was a building contractor, and she believed that his lack of involvement in housework and child care was due to his own orientation toward a traditional division of labor. He would rather she quit selling real estate than to help her with housework and child care:

> That's a source of stress in our marriage. I'm pretty much responsible for

the child care and the cooking, unless we get something at [carry out] or something like that. We do that probably three nights a week. His big thing is "Stay home, stay home and take care of the children."

This gender ideology is the most plausible explanation for some of the husbands who did not differ in any apparent way from the husbands who participated at a high level. Kendra Jones said that her husband did not cook or clean the house because "He doesn't consider that his job. He has never done that." His support consisted mainly of not complaining if she did not get all of the housework done:

> He'll say, "Let's go out to eat" if I've worked for two solid days on a weekend. And he definitely has never demanded that the house be clean or the clothes are clean or anything like that. And he'll try to do an errand for me.

For the most part, the type of housework that the women described their husbands as doing was consistent with other studies of the division of household labor.[23] Husbands' housework was confined generally to a narrow range of tasks—some meal preparation, staying with the children, putting them to bed—and only when the wives were working in the evenings or on weekends. When husbands increased their contributions to housework, it tended to be within this range. The husbands did not take on the major burdens of housecleaning, grocery and/or clothes shopping, clothing maintenance and the rest of what makes up the full load of household labor.

The women realtors reflected society's normative expectations about the gendered division of labor in families: although they were contributing to the economic support of their families, they retained responsibility for the household labor. They described their husbands' contributions to housework and child care as "helping" them, and were grateful for that help. Sandra Berry articulated this perspective on husbands' contributions to the second shift:

> He'll do anything I ask him to do, but he doesn't see [what needs to be done]. He'll do the laundry, if I leave a note: "A load in the dryer, a load in the wash, please do that," and then sometimes I'll even have to call him to remind him again. He'll do it, he's willing, he just has a short attention span. He tries.

Sandra's account reflects her own gender ideology as well as her perception of her husband's. She describes him as willing to "do anything I ask him to do," meaning that she is responsible for deciding what needs to be done and then telling him to do it. Her view of her husband is condescending in this quotation: "He just has a short attention span." Clearly, he is "helping" her, not quite sharing in the true sense of having mutual responsibility for the work. If the housework did not get done, the women felt that it was their fault. If the husbands were too busy or unwilling to participate, it was the wives' responsibility to find a way to get it done.

Husbands might also provide emotional support, which was important for many women. Tonia Marks believed that such support was essential:

> My husband is great at providing me with emotional support, which you need in this business. People just hammer on you, day after day. If you do not have a husband who is willing to work with you in this career, you will not make it. Or you will have great discontent, and marriage breakup and all that sort of stuff.

Several women spoke of high rates of marital stress and divorce among women realtors. They attributed this to the heavy demands of the work, especially the evening and weekend hours required, and the husbands' lack of understanding and support, emotionally and instrumentally, in sharing the household labor. Five of the women in this study were divorced or separated in 1990. Three of these women had been divorced before they started selling real estate. Only one of the other two attributed her separation to the strains associated with her real estate work. Thus, in the original sample, the relationship between the work and divorce did not apply. However, many of the still-married women acknowledged that their work was a source of conflict with their husbands.

By 1998, three more women were divorced, and two of the ones who had divorced between 1990 and 1998 blamed their work for the breakup of their marriages. Tess White, quoted previously, had alluded to this sort of conflict. I shall discuss the respondents' perception of a high rate of divorce among realtors in chapter 6, under the topic of the emotional costs of real estate sales work. I mention it here only as an example of the need for husbands' emotional support as well as sharing of household labor.

## Other Sources of Household Labor Power

In addition to, or in place of, their husbands' participation in housework and child care, many of the women relied on other forms of household help. Half of the women hired domestic workers who came in once a week or every other week to do housework.

For those whose husbands shared little of the family-related work, a combination of other forms of help was essential. For example Jennifer Gordon, whose husband worked eighty hours a week and who, she said had no time for child care and housework, relied on her mother and on paid domestic workers:

> I have a housekeeper who comes in from two to six [P.M.] every day. And she does the laundry and watches the children and cooks supper and keeps the house clean . . . [my] mother lives close by, and if I have an appointment [after the housekeeper's hours], I can either drop the children at her house, or she will come up here and stay with them.

Jennifer's arrangement represented the most extensive use of paid household assistance. Many of the other respondents had a cleaning service for one day, but no one else had a daily housekeeper/babysitter. Of the nine women with preschool-age children in 1990, eight used some form of paid child care. These forms included day-care centers and baby-sitters who kept children in their homes or who came to the child's home for weekday care, and in the evenings or on weekends when husbands were not available. The ninth woman relied entirely on her husband, mother, and mother-in-law to care for the children.

Among the fifteen women with children between five and twelve years of age, only one sent her children to an after-school day-care program, and one (Jennifer Gordon) had a baby-sitter meet the children at home. The others tried to be at home when their children got out of school, or relied on their husbands and/or the children's grandmothers to be with the children when the women were working. The mothers with school-age children had to make additional arrangements during school holidays and summer vacations. They cut back on their work hours to be with their children during those times, and used baby-sitters when necessary.

Finally, the women relied on technology to help them balance work and family responsibilities. The nature of real estate work determined the kinds of technology that were helpful. For example, most had cellular phones to enable them to take care of business as they drove or did housework and to stay in touch with their families while they worked. All had answering machines or "voice mail boxes" to record telephone calls when they were busy. Tonia Marks described her system of deferring calls during family time:

> I have two phone lines. The first phone line has call forwarding. So I always forward that into my voice mail box [during dinner]. Line two is the family phone. If for some reason I forget to put it [call forwarding] on, my

children answer the phone, and they'll say "Mom's eating dinner." Unless it's something I know I'm really waiting for.

Some were reluctant to ignore any calls if they were at home and could hear the phone. For example, Colleen Ewing said that she could not restrain herself from answering the phone anytime it rang:

> Everybody tells me to put my calls on forward for that [family] time. But I will never, I can't do that. I'm afraid that someone will have an anxiety attack over a house they just bought, or someone will have a question that can't wait. . . . If someone calls in the middle of dinner, I will take the phone call. I shouldn't, but I do.

Such reluctance was more typical of those who had been in the business a lesser amount of time. As they gained experience and confidence they were more likely to agree with Tonia, that phone calls could wait if they were busy with family activities.

## Boundary Work

The women realtors illustrate two points about boundary work, the ways of negotiating the relationship between home and work. First, the fact that they hold a variety of ideas about the appropriate mix of home and work demonstrates the arbitrary character of people's perceptions of the permeability of the boundaries between the two realms. Second, the effects of spouses' attitudes and work arrangements, and the needs of children on their work arrangements demonstrate the structural constraints within which individuals make decisions about the relationship between work and home.

People draw the line between their home lives and their work lives along a continuum from total segmentation, in which there is no overlap, to total integration, in which there is no distinction between the two realms. Three factors influence the individual's decision about this relationship.[25] Each of these factors affects the ways that realtors combine their work with their families.

The first factor is the way one has been socialized to view home and work. The internalized meanings of "home" and "work" that result from socialization would influence one's choice of real estate sales as an occupation: the individual who becomes a realtor is likely to fall closer to the integrationist end of the continuum. The appeal of the work is its flexibility and its "personal" nature—the necessity of working closely with people in an emotional decision-making process (see chapter 6 for the factors that attract people to this work.) Also, each woman brings her ingrained ideas of how work and family should relate to each other. These ideas come from what she experienced as a child—how her parents and other adults around her negotiated the boundaries between work and home—and what she was told was the appropriate relationship. Socialization continues into adulthood, as changing conditions and experiences alter one's definitions of what is appropriate (e.g., a woman who starts selling real estate with the intention of keeping her sales work separate from her home life might find that she can make business calls while supervising her children's homework, and gradually soften her ideas about the boundaries between the two domains.)

A second factor that helps to determine how a person defines the appropriate relationship between home and work is the ways that one's home and work are structured and the expectations of other people in both realms. Although it is possible to segment this kind of work from one's personal life, many factors mitigate against such a strategy. The fact that a realtor works odd hours, and has frequent "down time" between appointments and other work-related obligations, makes it awkward to be in either realm completely. The focus of their work—selling private residences—reinforces the ties between home and work. They are *in* and thinking *about* homes for much of their work time. Although not their own homes, the work/home connections are hard to ignore as a realtor.

The third factor in determining one's position on the continuum between integration and segmentation is the personal boundary-producing practices that one adopts to delineate home and work. The descriptions by the respondents of how they schedule their days and meet the obligations of both domains demonstrate how far each goes in integrating their real estate work with their homework. These descriptions are full of examples of segmentation and integration: Tonia Marks has two phone lines—one for the family, one for work—clearly a segmenting device. Sandra Berry returns her business calls in the car with her family, an extremely integrated mode of living. Thus, the different practices that result from differing perspectives on the relationship between home and work end up influencing that relationship.

The women recognized that their interests and obligations at home affected their ability to perform well in their jobs, and most felt that the effect was more negative than positive. When asked if they thought that their family obligations had had any effect on their work opportunities, many said that they believed the effect had been negative, that they could have worked more and been more successful economically if they had not had family obligations. They were competing with men and other women who did not have family obligations, and felt disadvantaged.

By 1998 many of the respondents no longer had young children at home, and were feeling that the result was less stress and more productivity in their work. Tonia Marx for example said that although she had always been able to sell a lot of houses because of her cooperative family, she now had more time for herself:

> It has given me more "Tonia time." I am choosing to take more time away from work and do things like an aerobics class or a weekend seminar. I am doing this for me. I don't have to worry about [the children].

Deborah Engels, in comparing her life in 1990 and 1998, agreed that

> It was difficult [in 1990 and before that] with my daughter being young. Now she's in college and I don't have to worry about any of that. I have more time and, well, less stress. I don't feel like I have to rush home between three and four o'clock. Of course, that did change as she got a little older, that time got a little later. Then my obligation was to make sure that dinner was on the table. Now I don't have to worry about that at all.

In contrast to the "profile" of the successful realtor that was described for another study in 1986 (see above), several women said that they had been told, and had come to believe, that the ideal residential salesperson would be a divorced woman with grown children because, as Deborah Engels explained,

> As a former wife who had raised children, she'd know how to manage time and money, as a woman she'd understand houses and people, but she'd no longer be distracted from business by family obligations. And since she's divorced, she'd work hard to support herself.

I found this shift in ideas of the "perfect" residential salesperson fascinating. It could represent geographic differences within the industry or modifications resulting from repeated telling (like the children's game of "gossip" in which a line whispered successively to a circle of listeners comes back to the original teller in a wildly distorted version.) But it could be that the latter "profile" represents changes in thinking within the field over time, reflecting the observations and experiences of women in both categories. It describes a more segmented type of boundary work than did the earlier description, of a woman with children and a husband who would provide compatible pressures and expectations. But perhaps it merely reflects more accurately the obstacles to integration—the demands of the work are often in conflict with the demands of the family and cannot simply be shoved together.

In her more recent book, *The Time Bind*, Arlie Hochschild found that parents were employing a strategy for balancing work and family life that she calls "emotionally downsizing."[26] They were spending less time doing family work and more at their jobs, and convincing themselves that family needs were fewer than they had once assumed. I don't know if this strategy applied to any of my respondents; it simply did not occur to me to question them about their perceptions of family needs, and the quotation that opens this chapter reinforced my assumption that family needs were not negotiable. Kendra Jones says that women can only become "obsessed" with the work if they do not have families; thus, she negates any possibility of emotionally downsizing one's family's needs. But this sort of rationalization of increasing one's focus on work resonates in the quotation about the perfect salesperson, who has no family distractions to keep her from her work. It is also a strategy that results in more segmentation between work and home.

In conclusion, the work of selling real estate requires a greater time commitment and more adaptations in the arrangements for household labor than the women anticipated. It has been a contention of this chapter that women feel conflict between their paid and family work, because they have been socialized to perceive housework and child care as their responsibilities. Adding intense involvement in a demanding career increases the level of stress and contradictions in women's lives, levels higher than most women probably experienced in the past. In the next chapter, we shall examine the relationship of gender to the experience of doing real estate sales work.

## Notes

1. Riika Kivimaki, "Work and Parenthood," in *Gendered Practices in Working Life*, eds. Liisa Rantalaiho and Tuula Heiskanen (New York: St. Martin's Press, 1997), 99.

2. Dana Dunn, *Workplace, Women's Place: An Anthology* (Los Angeles: Roxbury Press, 1997), 9.

3. Kivimaki, "Work and Parenthood," 89.

4. Sarah F. Berk, "Women's Unpaid Labor: Home and Community," in *Women Working: Theories and Facts in Perspective*, 2nd edition, eds. Anne Helton Stromberg and Shirley Harkess (Mountain View, Calif.: Mayfield, 1988); Toni M. Calasanti and Carol A. Bailey, "Gender Inequality and the Division of Household Labor in the United States and Sweden: A Socialist-Feminist Approach," *Social Problems* 38, no. 1 (February 1991): 34-53; Shelley Coverman, "Role Overload, Role Conflict, and Stress: Addressing Consequences of Multiple-Role Demands," *Social Forces* 67, no. 3 (June 1989): 965-982; Beth Anne Shelton, "The Distribution of Household Tasks: Does Wife's Employment Make a Difference?" *Journal of Family Issues* 11, no. 2 (June 1990): 115-135.

5. Arlie Hochschild, *The Second Shift: Working Parents and the Revolution at Home* (New York: Viking Press, 1989); Arlie Hochschild, *The Time Bind: When Work Becomes Home and Home Becomes Work* (New York: Metropolitan Books, 1997); Dorothy E. Smith, "Women's Inequality and the Family" in *Families and Work*, eds. Naomi Gerstel and Harriet Engel Gross (Philadelphia, Pa.: Temple University Press, 1987), 23-54.

6. Hochschild, *The Second Shift,* 1989.

7. Jeanne M. Brett and Sara Yogev, "Restructuring Work for Family: How Dual-Earner Couples with Children Manage," in *Work and Family: Theory, Research, and Applications*, ed. Elizabeth B. Goldsmith (Newbury Park, Calif.: Sage Publications, 1989), 159-174.

8. April A. Brayfield and Sandra L. Hofferth, "Employment Schedules and Sharing Child Care: Dual-Earner Couples in the United States," paper presented at the annual meeting of the Southern Sociological Society, Atlanta, Ga., April 1991; Harriet B. Presser, "Shift Work and Child Care Among Young Dual-Earner American Parents," *Journal of Marriage and the Family* 50, no. 1 (February 1988): 133-148.

9. Dorothy E. Smith, *The Everyday World as Problematic: A Feminist Sociology* (Boston: Northeastern University Press, 1987).

10. William T. Bielby and Denise D. Bielby, "Family Ties: Balancing Commitments to Work and Family in Dual Earner Households," *American Sociological Review* 54, no. 5 (October 1989): 776-789; Eileen Boris, "Homework and Women's Rights: The Case of the Vermont Knitters, 1980-1985," *Signs: Journal of Women in Culture and Society* 13, no. 1 (fall 1987): 98-120; Karyn Loscocco and Joyce Robinson, "Barriers to Women's Small-Business Success in the United States," *Gender & Society* 5, no. 4 (December 1991): 511-532.

11. Jane Aronson, "Women's Sense of Responsibility for the Care of Old People: But Who Else is Going to do it?" *Gender & Society* 6, no. 1 (March 1992): 8-29; Janet Chafetz, "The Gender Division of Labor and the Reproduction of Female Disadvantage," *Journal of Family Issues* 9, no. 1 (March 1988): 103-31; Janet G. Hunt and Larry L. Hunt, "The Dualities of Careers and Families: New Integrations

or New Polarizations?" *Social Problems* 29, no. 5 (June 1982): 499-510.

12. Evelyn Nakano Glenn, "From Servitude to Service Work: Historical Continuities in the Racial Division of Paid Reproductive Labor," *Signs: Journal of Women in Culture and Society* 18, no. 1 (fall 1992): 1-43.

13. Barbara J. Thomas and Barbara F. Reskin, "A Woman's Place is Selling Homes: Occupational Change and the Feminization of Real Estate Sales," in *Job Queues, Gender Queues: Explaining Women's Inroads into Male Occupations*, eds Barbara F. Reskin and Patricia A. Roos (Philadelphia, Pa.: Temple University Press, 1990), 205-223.

14. See, for example, Judith S. McIlwee and J. Gregg Robinson, *Women in Engineering: Gender, Power, and Workplace Culture* (New York: State University of New York Press, 1992); Rosemary Pringle, *Secretaries Talk: Sexuality, Power and Work* (London: Verso, 1989); Ellen I. Rosen, *Bitter Choices: Blue-Collar Women in and out of Work* (Chicago: University of Chicago Press,1989).

15. Thomas and Reskin, "A Woman's Place is Selling Homes," 1990, 216.

16. Thomas and Reskin, "A Woman's Place is Selling Homes," 1990.

17. Hochschild, *The Second Shift*, 1989.

18. Interestingly, Tonia also mentioned her husband's help with her real estate work, picking up papers (contracts), putting up For Sale signs, compiling lists of phone numbers of people to contact. Other women also mentioned these sorts of help from their husbands and children.

19. See, for example, Berk, "Women's Unpaid Labor," 1988; Calasanti and Bailey, "Gender Inequality and the Division of Household Labor in the United States and Sweden," 1991; Hochschild, *The Second Shift*, 1989; Jeanne Miller and Howard H. Garrison, "Sex Roles: The Division of Labor at Home and in the Workplace," *Annual Review of Sociology* 8 (1982): 237-262; Shelton, "The Distribution of Household Tasks," 1991.

20. Hochschild (*The Second Shift*, 1989) found this sort of "wishful thinking" among her respondents, who often claimed that they were splitting housework more evenly than her observations revealed.

21. Caroline Dryden, *Being Married, Doing Gender: A Critical Analysis of Gender Relationships in Marriage* (New York: Routledge, 1999).

22. Hunt and Hunt, "The Dualities of Careers and Families," 1982.

23. See, for example, Berk, "Women's Unpaid Labor," 1988.

24. Christena E. Nippert-Eng, *Home and Work: Negotiating Boundaries Through Everyday Life* (Chicago: The University of Chicago Press, 1996), 6.

25. Nippert-Eng, *Home and Work*, 1996, 6.

26. Hochschild, *The Time Bind*, 1997.

## Chapter Five

# Real Estate Sales Work as Gender Work

[G]ender [is] an institution that establishes patterns of expectations for individuals, orders the social processes of everyday life, is built into the major social organizations of society . . . gender is one of the major ways that human beings organize their lives. . . . What is dubbed "women's work" or "men's work" has a sense of normality and naturalness, an almost moral quality, even though the justification for such typification is usually an after-the-fact rationalization.
—**Judith Lorber**, *Paradoxes of Gender*[1]

I think women make far better realtors: patience, understanding, sympathy, compassion. Those things you may not think come into play in real estate, but they're really very important. Just attitude, to sum it up. Men are very, don't really hear, they're never really thinking about what you're saying, always thinking about the next thing they want to do. . . . Generally speaking, of course. And they will not do their work. When you're the listing agent and there's a man who's the selling agent, nine times out of ten they don't take care of the details that need to be done. I just think women are better at this job.
—**Elizabeth Rivers**, six years in real estate

What does being female or male have to do with selling real estate? Since both women and men excel at this work, it would seem that gender is irrelevant. And yet, women are far more likely to be found in residential sales than in commercial, to be sales agents rather than brokers, and to work under the legal protection of a broker/manager rather than to form their own agency. Furthermore, as the quotation above indicates, many women believe that their gender enhances their abilities as realtors.

The general assumption in the literature on gender in the workplace is that gendering is imposed, on women at least, by the force of social convention and masculine hegemony. In this view, gendering is embraced by men to preserve their place in the hierarchy, but rejected by women who have more to gain by neutralizing gender expectations. For example, Patricia Y. Martin and David L. Collinson refer to a process in which men managers "mobilize masculinity" in their values and practices to exclude women.[2] Yet, the women whom I interviewed also seemed to mobilize femininity and to incorporate an understanding of gender into their definitions of themselves as realtors.

Gender is a meaning system that develops at the individual level as well as the institutional level. Recent feminist research emphasizes that gender is not a static dichotomy—male and female—but a dynamic complex of statuses interacting with race, ethnicity, and social class to produce vast differences in power and opportunity. The focus of gender scholarship in the past decade has been to question the concept of gender itself, the categories "women" and "men": what process creates these categories and makes them socially meaningful.

The construction of gender is a "lifelong work in progress."[3] Rather than a set of norms and roles imposed on the individual by society, gender is a product of the interactions between the society's expectations and the individual's modifications and enactments of those expectations. As agents of their own gender construction, individuals support or challenge the gender divisions of a society.[4] The construction of gender occurs at all levels of society, from the micro to the macro, from the individual's experiences to the society's cultural practices.

The interrelationships of gender, work, and identity in occupational settings make such settings loci for gender production and reproduction.[5] Thus, people construct gender as workers, and individuals contribute to their own gender identity by their actions as women or men within their occupational field. Workers may emphasize the relevance of gender in their work, by claiming that women or men are better at a specific job, or de-emphasize its relevance by asserting that a woman can perform the job as well as a man can.[6]

In gender-segregated occupations, workers and employers selectively identify job characteristics as affirming masculinity or femininity. Such determinations are highly variable, yet they serve as rationales for gender segregation and enable individuals to interpret their work as most suitable for their own gender, and thus reconcile their work with an identity they can accept.[7]

The traditional corporation has been identified as "a man's world." Social traits that our society associates with men, such as aggressive individualism, instrumentalism, independence and competition, are regarded as important for success and are rewarded by advancement up the corporate ladder. Women who succeed in the corporate world do so by conforming to the "masculine" model. They exhibit characteristics that are accepted in our society as masculine: toughness, independence, willingness to take risks, and ambition.[8]

On the other hand, organizations such as *Ms.* magazine, that define themselves as valuing women's abilities, deliberately develop non-hierarchical work structures that encourage relationships based on nurturance and participatory decision making.[9] Many network direct selling organizations are organized in similar ways, emphasizing interpersonal encouragement and cooperation. DSOs such as Mary Kay Cosmetics and Tupperware, whose distributors are almost exclusively women, could be categorized as "feminine" organizations.

Unlike these predominantly gender segregated workforces, real estate salespeople include high percentages of both women and men, making this field apparently gender neutral. Rather than focusing on the ways that definitions of appropriate gender behavior may be framed to explain gender segregation, this chapter analyzes the ways that workers themselves perceive gender as relevant to their jobs. The nature of real estate sales work, where individual salespeople work independently and usually alone, means that the workers are not in close proximity to each other for most of the work day. They do not form a workplace culture that resembles organizations where workers, predominantly male or female, are together all day. In those settings, workers often bond together by constructing gender as an important characteristic of the job. Thus, printers have claimed that only men could be typesetters because women are not physically strong enough to handle heavy type.[10] On the shop floor, male workers employ discourses that privilege experiences—being the family breadwinner, able to swear and joke "like a man," unemotional—as a way of constructing a shared sense of masculine identity. But even in nonsegregated situations, workers tailor notions of proper gender enactment to suit their own experiences. In spite of the flexibility of definitions of proper gender enactment, individuals are able to articulate a clear description of how their gender relates to their job.

The data provide several ways of examining the significance of gender in the work experiences of the women realtors. First, do they believe that their gender affects their opportunities in this field, and if so, are the effects positive or negative? Second, do the women believe that gender makes a difference in how they experience their work, regardless of how they feel about their opportunities? Third, do they perceive resistance from men to the increasing presence of women in the occupation? Finally, do they use gender to explain women's concentration in residential sales and relatively low representation in commercial real estate? My focus in this chapter is on the significance of gender for workers who could presumably ignore gender in their work roles.

My argument is not that women (or men) cling to gendered practices in some simplistic sort of self-defeating behavior. Rather, the combination of expectations that surround an individual in her life as worker, wife, mother, and so on makes it probable that she will reproduce gendered practices in all of her roles. And the effect of that reproduction is that she will have limitations on her work opportunities that her male colleagues do not have. By looking at the women's perceptions of the significance of gender in their work experiences, this chapter contributes to an understanding of the interactive and subjective nature of gender construction.

## Organizing by Gender

Nationally, women realtors have considered gender sufficiently important to their work that they have formed a caucus for themselves. The Women's Council of Realtors (WCR) is a national organization with state and local chapters. The WCR sponsors public service events, professional development programs, lobbying the state legislature, and social events designed to facilitate networking among realtors. Although the organization is open to men and women, it was founded with gender-specific objectives: "providing a place for women in the industry to learn from each other," as Casey Burns said. Fiona Miller provided more details, explaining that the council offers a network, an information source, and a way to get involved:

> When I first came into real estate someone said, "Why don't we go to a [WCR] meeting" and I went and it was one of those things where, there was a whole room full of professional women. I didn't want to be just a little housewife who sold three houses a year. I wanted this to be my profession. And I was really impressed with the women who were there—high power. There are some men who come. It's not closed to just women. It started out

being women, because women didn't have a way of learning or knowing anything. The men would go out on the golf course, or in the locker room, and hear about the old boy network, but women didn't really have a way of learning about different things.

So I joined, started going to the meetings. They meet once a month, educational meetings. It might be about new financing; each month it was something different, always with an outside speaker. It got to be a networking, a way of meeting realtors and people in the mortgage business.

It's really fun, because there are a lot of times when we get together and just have luncheons or whatever, just a fun type of thing. Which is good, because you get to meet other people. And it's great to pick up the phone and say, "Hi, Sue, can I show your listing on . . ." instead of not knowing the listing agent. Or calling and asking questions about a house.

Fiona's explanation is rife with gender-referenced reasons for joining the WCR. Just the fact that she found it important to associate with other women realtors meant that she saw being a woman in this field as a distinct experience. She was impressed at her first WCR meeting by the women who were present because they were "professional" and "high power." She was anxious not to be perceived as a "little housewife" selling very little, which apparently was her impression of how women appeared who were not sufficiently "professional." I never heard anyone describe how a man with a low sales volume would be perceived, and I can think of no male stereotype that is comparable to the "little housewife." Fiona's perspective reflects her consciousness of gender as a factor in her work experiences.

Fiona's perspective was a minority one, however, in regard to the positive importance of the WCR. The local WCR chapter had fewer than three hundred members, including both women and men, and represented a small percentage of the area's realtors. Most of my respondents did not belong, although a few were active and one was a past president of the local chapter. In explaining why they did not belong, most said they simply did not have time, but a few said they did not want to belong to a women's organization because they felt that it promoted a ghettoization of women in the profession. Even Fiona felt that the name "sounds like we're against men or something," and the local chapter had discussed changing their name to The Council so that more people would become involved. Laura Howell explained that although the WCR had "actively recruited" her a number of times, her previous involvement in women's organizations when she worked in a bank made her leery of joining the WCR:

I was really involved with a number of women's organizations and what I found was that the men really resented the fact that women banded together. I found out that men referred to the National Association of Bank Women, NABW, as the National Association of Bunny Wabbits. And I just decided when I left banking that I would no longer associate myself with purely female organizations because I think it's counterproductive.

Laura's perspective contrasted sharply with Fiona Miller's. Laura did not look to women realtors as her role models, and felt that organizations such as the WCR placed too much emphasis on gender and were therefore "counterproductive." When I asked her to clarify her meaning, she said that the WCR separated women and men and caused resentment of women by men. While Fiona found networking with women valuable, Laura preferred to network with other *realtors*, regardless of gender categories.

The majority of respondents agreed that the WCR had a derogatory reputation, and/or that it was primarily a social organization that accomplished little professionally. However, many of the women who did not want to join the WCR saw their gender as significant to their career. While they did not feel a need to join formally with other women in the occupation, they recognized the fact that they experienced the work *as women*, that gender was salient to their colleagues and their customers. They simply preferred not to emphasize gender anymore than necessary. They saw the significance of gender as both an asset and a liability.

This finding seems at first consideration to contradict the sentiments of women like Laura Howell, who did not want to emphasize gender by joining female organizations and in fact, Laura was consistent in her denial that gender had any effect on her work as a realtor. However, she represented only twenty percent of the respondents in taking this absolutist position.

In seeking an explanation for the differences between Fiona and Laura, and the other respondents who agreed with one or the other, I found that gender consciousness was the most compelling factor. I do not believe that the women constructed their own gender identities in significantly different ways. They dressed similarly, performed the roles of wife and mother similarly, clearly defined themselves as women. The difference lay in their awareness of themselves as members of a gender category that separates them from men: Fiona saw that membership as an important part of her identity; Laura did not. In her answers to other questions about gender in her work, Laura consistently denied that being a woman had had any effect on her experiences. Fiona, and the majority of the other respondents, saw and articulated various ways that gender affected their work.

## Gender as Asset

In response to the question of whether or not they perceived that being women had affected their work opportunities in any way, eighty percent said that it had. While many felt that the effects had been both positive and negative, more cited advantages to being a woman realtor than cited disadvantages.[11]

The respondents were active agents in constructing their identities as women realtors. While they have participated in undermining the former status quo of their occupation, which privileged men as sales agents, they have redefined the occupation as one in which gender is still an important category of difference in the individual's experiences as a realtor.

For the majority, who believed that their gender was an advantage in residential sales work, being women meant that they brought particular skills and insights to the work of selling houses. The perceived advantages related to two issues: the belief that customers preferred women as sales agents, and the women's own conviction that they were better than men at selling residential real estate. Both of these reasons are based on the women's selection of job characteristics that they defined as compatible with their proper enactment of gender. Specifically, they focused on two areas of expertise that they felt were most important in selling houses: emotion work and knowledge of the product. Ellie Denton, who worked as a site agent in a large development of higher-priced, custom-built new homes, felt that she had seen enough female and male realtors to describe some gender differences:

> I come into contact with probably twenty or thirty agents a week, and at least half of them are men. The men are totally in it for the business. A lot of women, I feel, are in it for more of a way of life and doing things. I don't know how to describe it, I just get a different feeling. The men are there with clients, to sell them a house and get the hell rid of them. Women are there, and I know this is how I am, I get involved with the couple. If they tell me a sad story, it makes me sad. If they tell me a happy story, it makes me happy. Whereas if they have a man agent there, he'll be like, "Ok, that's good. Now let's go over here and look at this one."
>
> Women have that extra touch in real estate, and I think they make better real estate agents, personally. Because they go into the house and if the wife is talking about this, this, and this, a man real estate agent, I don't think any of that stuff clicks. They just think, "What else could you possibly want?" Whereas a woman is saying to me things like "I want to make sure I have this microwave here, located here, at this height," and I could think of plans

which had the layout of the kitchen exactly like she wanted. Working with a lot of men real estate agents, they bring in clients [and] I can hear what they [the clients] are saying to me, but their agent is ignoring them. He just doesn't want to take time. It goes over his head.

Ellie's description of the difference between women and men realtors includes the qualities that other respondents agreed were gender related: Men are more "businesslike," unemotional, oblivious to their clients' feelings. Women are concerned with their clients as *people*, and are sensitive to the emotions and events that affect these people. Women listen to the clients' stories and are less concerned with making a quick sale than with matching people to the houses that fit them best. Women know what people prefer in housing designs and are familiar with various floor plans that match those preferences. Thus, women are superior in meeting their customers need and giving them expert advice on housing. As a result of these differences, Ellie believed that clients would rather work with her and that she was a better realtor than most of the men she had observed.

I found that the women mentioned emotional labor, the work of managing feelings—one's own and those of one's customers—most frequently as being gender-related. Rather than being subject to their emotions, women in our culture are socialized to be more adept than men at managing their emotions in the service of affirming and/or enhancing the well-being of others. Jobs involving emotional labor comprise twice as many of all jobs that women do as jobs that men do.[12] Emotion work is expected of women and gender stereotypes result in the assumption that women will be responsible for comforting and making others feel comfortable. The respondents saw buying and selling houses as emotional experiences for most customers. The emotion work involved in persuading clients to buy a house and helping them feel good about their decisions meant that the realtor must separate her personal feelings from her professional demeanor, and manage the emotion-charged experiences of clients. For example, Tess White described her success in selling real estate as related to being a woman:

> I honestly feel that I can do a better job than most men in real estate. Real estate is an emotional process; it is not a dollars and cents process. I understand the more emotional side. . . . I would have to say that if you look at the top producers, they're women.[13]

In addition to defining themselves as more sensitive to customers' emotions, respondents believed women excel at residential sales because they are better than men at making decorating suggestions and at relating to women customers, whom they believed are more often the principal decision makers in buying houses. As Laura Howell stated:

> The wives make the buying decisions. The husband's gonna make the finance decision, in most cases, but the choice of homes is made by the wives, and it's easier for them to relate to female agents.

Furthermore, the respondents argued that women *see* the product—the house for sale—differently, and are more in tune with their customers' perceptions. Houses are the sites of family life, requiring sufficient space arranged to facilitate all of the activities of people at various life stages. Allison Foote's explanation of why women can relate better to customers than men can is a typical example:

> For me and for most women, we can go in and look at a house, and point out all of the things about that house that make it wonderful, that can relate to another woman, because we're seeing it through a woman's eyes—a kitchen with these nice counter spaces, and so on.

Finally, several respondents said women were well-suited to selling houses because they pay attention to the details involved in closing a sale better than do men, and handle stress better. In all these respects, the women saw gender as an asset in their work.

Most of the women, then, did see their success and satisfaction with the job as gender-related and gender affirming. There were a few respondents, however, who had experienced negative reactions to women as realtors.

## Gender as Liability

Those women who felt that their gender had been a liability in this occupation agreed that gender-based differences gave women an advantage in satisfying the job requirements, but felt that customers and male realtors were blocking, or trying to block, women from successfully accomplishing the tasks. They had encountered customers or salesmen—usually only one or two—who were unwilling to work with women. Often, these were older men, as in the following account by Beth Tripp:

> I have found that, with my special area being older homes, frequently I come across older sellers. An eighty-year-old man getting ready to sell a

house still thinks that a woman's place is *in* the home. She knows nothing about business and she has no business selling a house. And he would never list his house with a woman. . . . So I call a [male] coworker and I say, "Ok, you go list the house. This guy's not going to list with me. You get the listing and then I'll do my share to sell it." And then we split the commission.

Beth's example is hypothetical, although it is based on her experiences. She has encountered an attitude, usually among older men, but it could also have been among older couples or men younger than eighty, that she believed was based on gender bias. She could only recall two times when it had happened, and she had dealt with it as she describes, by retreating from the listing and recruiting a male colleague to serve as her "front man." None of the other respondents were as specific, although several said that they had encountered older customers, male and female, who were reluctant to work with them, and they attributed the hesitation to gender bias.

In addition to resistance from customers, women realtors sometimes encountered resistance from male realtors, as the following incident, recounted by Chris Harden, illustrates:

Three or four years ago I showed a house for a man [a listing agent] during, of all things, hunting season. Everytime I'd call his office I'd get "He's out hunting." So I wasn't even sure that the house was still available. But I went ahead and showed it, and I wrote the contract. I could tell from the first time he finally called that he did not want to deal with me. And I knew that it was because I was a woman. I don't think he came right out and said it. I think it was the tone of his voice, his attitude and so on. I always do my job as thoroughly and completely as I possibly can, and when it was all over he called me up and said, "I realize I was a little hard on you when you brought me that contract, but you conducted your business beautifully and I'll be happy to work with you again." And I thought that probably took a lot on his part to admit he had been kind of an ogre to start with.

This story illustrates an important point about how gender influences experiences. Chris had no evidence that gender had any effect on the male agent's behavior toward her, but she was certain that it was significant. In most cases, as with Chris Harden, the women felt that they had proven themselves capable and had overcome the individual's resistance, but that they would encounter other men with the same attitudes/prejudices.

In examining relationships with male colleagues, almost all of the women said that they had experienced resentment or discrimination from male realtors at some time in their careers. However, most felt that such attitudes were held by only a small percentage of men. One of the most common attitudes that the women had encountered from men was that women were not as serious in sales work as men, that women were working for "pocket money," rather than to support their families, as men were. For example, Sandra Berry knew of one man who,

> Sometimes when he goes for a listing he'll tell them he has to sell their house, he has three boys at home, mouths to feed, and his wife doesn't work. "You know I'll work for you. I'm not just a woman going out for a tea party."

The women resented this assumption that they were not as highly motivated as men were. Other male agents seemed to believe that women knew less about the technical aspects of construction and sales.[14] The women said that they countered both of these forms of discrimination—the assumption that they deserve less business because they are not working as hard and the belief that they do not know as much about real estate—by proving themselves hard working and knowledgeable.

Some respondents believed there was a correlation between the men's attitudes and their ages: that older men were more resistant to women's participation in the field. Others found no such relationship, but felt that less successful men were more likely to blame women for taking business away from them. In these cases, women become the scapegoats for men's lack of success.

The strategies for overcoming the liabilities of gender in all of these cases involved downplaying gender. Instead of emphasizing the strengths that they believe they have as women in the field, the women avoided calling attention to gender and tried to prove that they were "as good as" a man. Thus, Chris Harden never mentioned the apparent prejudice of the male listing agent, but worked hard to make the sale and show him that she could do well. And Beth Tripp did not attempt to convince a reluctant client to work with her. She worked behind the scenes with a male colleague as her "front man." This minimalization is just another of the diverse and sometimes contradictory ways that individuals enact gender. The individual's construction of gender identity at work occurs in a context of power differences that frequently necessitate shifting definitions and presentations of self. When gender becomes a liability because of the gender definitions of others, particularly others with power over the individual, then the individual may present herself or himself in a way that downplays gender.

## Gender as Difference

The second question concerning gender focused on whether women's experiences in real estate sales differed from men's experiences. All of the respondents, even those who had stated that gender had not affected their work opportunities, gave examples of how they perceived women's and men's experiences to be different. Most of the differences that the women described did not concern discrete events but different ways of *experiencing* their work. For example, Tess White made the following observation:

> I think in new construction, builders feel that men know more about construction of a home—the studs, the rafters, insulation. And a lot of builders [believe] that women understand the frilly curtains and the color scheme. And it may be that if you took a test of men and a test of women, I would probably say that men understand more about construction. That's probably true. But that's not to say a woman isn't capable of understanding.

In another sense of difference, respondents felt that men were less interested in the buyers as families, as Kendra Jones explained:

> I've noticed in the office, a man [agent] will come in, they don't want kids in their car. I was talking to a new [male] agent Sunday, and I had come in with a couple and they had a two-year-old [child] and he was running around and I gave him some paper and a pencil. And when they left he [the agent] said, "Whew! People who can't control their kids!" And I said, "Oh, I had two young ones recently all over my car and they wouldn't stay strapped in, and I was concerned about that" and he say, "Well, I'm not driving children around." I said, "Let me tell you something. Most of the people who buy houses have children." And he just looked at me and said, "I don't like children." He'll find out.

The descriptions here are packed with gender attributes, and these attributes are associated with successful real estate sales work. Women are assumed to be more emotional, more intuitive, more detail-oriented, more sensitive, better able to handle stress, better able to relate to women (who are, supposedly, the principal decision makers in family home buying), more patient, more empathetic.

These associations between gender attributes and successful work performance sound plausible: they have a commonsense ring of truth to them. They are, nevertheless, arbitrary designations—arbitrary in the sense of being identified "causes" of success in the occupation and arbitrary in the sense of being identified characteristics of women. These women believed that they had evidence that women were more likely than were men to possess these characteristics, but they were relying on stereotypes of women and men. These claims do not explain the fact that men continue to represent at least one third of residential sales people, or that men still outrank women in terms of sales volume.[15]

## Gender as Placement

Finally, gender attributes were employed to explain women's concentration in residential sales and relatively low representation in commercial real estate. A few respondents felt that commercial was not really open to women, that it is a field composed mostly of businessmen as clients and men as sales agents:

> In commercial you deal with a lot more bigwig types, and I think most of those people are men, in those positions, and they want to deal with other men.

And another woman said:

> I think it's a lot tougher for a female to break into the commercial field.... I think maybe the closed doors, it's a good-old-guy system.

For the most part, whether or not they perceived commercial real estate as a "man's world" that was resistant to admitting women, the respondents described commercial as less attractive to them than residential. They believed that women realtors in general did not want to sell commercial real estate, and argued that commercial was less flexible in terms of working hours. Since business had to be conducted during regular business hours, commercial agents were more tied to a nine-to-five, Monday through Friday work schedule than they preferred. They also believed that commercial dealt more with "nuts and bolts" issues, such as price per square foot and financing issues, whereas residential focused less on these concerns and more on the customers' personal preferences and emotional reactions/concerns.

Karen Horner was the only respondent who expressed any interest in entering the commercial field, and she felt that it would be a difficult transition for a woman:

> It's a man's world. I think they [women] are kept out of it. I talked to a commercial broker years ago because I thought maybe I'd like to go into commercial real estate at that point. And he told me, he was real blunt with me, he said, "You're going to get propositions. You're going to be asked to do a lot of things that you might not want to do to make something go, because you are a woman, because men just feel like they can do that." He was pretty explicit. In fact, I was talking to another commercial agent, a man, a couple of weeks ago, and I told him about when I talked to this other man, and he said, "You know something? It hasn't changed much in the last twelve years."

The commercial broker had, deliberately or unconsciously, invoked a stereotypical masculinity in his cautionary tale. He based his warning to Karen on an assumption that men in the commercial field would make sexual advances to her simply because she was a woman and "men just feel like they can do that." Although he was ostensibly speaking to her as a friend, he was mobilizing a masculinity that is hostile to women and protective of men's territory.

Finally, a rational explanation for why women were less likely to enter commercial than residential was that commercial requires a higher initial investment and a longer wait. According to Jennifer Gibson:

> Probably the main thing is in residential you tend to get your money a little bit faster. With commercial, it ties up a piece of property for a long time and there's a lot of expense involved, and it may set for months and months or a year without recouping any of the money.

While my group of respondents did not include any commercial agents, all of these respondents recognized the fact that some women choose commercial and do well in it. Nevertheless, they all used gender constructs as explanations for the lower proportion of women in commercial real estate.

In all of these ways, then, women who sell residential real estate construct identities for themselves based on their own definitions of gender, often asserting that their femininity is an asset in selling residential real estate. The women participants themselves engage in transforming real estate sales work into a job "suitable for a woman." They describe ways that being a woman is significant to their ways of being a realtor. In spite of statistical near-equality, and although most of the women in this study felt that opportunities in the field were similar for women and men, the respondents were able to enumerate job attributes that they perceived were related to gender, and to explain their own successes as at least partially gender-related.

For the most part, the women cite gender attributes that make them good realtors, rather than job characteristics that are compatible with gender. They invoke attributes that they believe are characteristic of themselves and of women in general to explain why they are well suited for their work. These attributes include patience, thoroughness, empathy with their customers, and an understanding of families' housing needs. To the outside observer, these traits may not seem particularly associated with women, but to the women realtors they serve as a rationale for the presence of a high percentage of women in the field.

Whether or not their clients agree with this perception of women realtors' special affinity for the work, the realtors appear convinced that gender is relevant to their work. However, most would not go so far as to claim that they chose to enter this occupation because they saw it as a woman's job. There were other, more pertinent reasons for selecting and enjoying this field. In the next chapter, we shall look at the women's assessment of the work, and with what in general makes a job "good" or "bad" to the workers themselves.

## Notes

1. Judith Lorber, *Paradoxes of Gender* (New Haven, Conn.: Yale University Press, 1994), 1, 15, 198.

2. Patricia Y. Martin and Donald L. Collinson, "Gender and Sexuality in Organizations," in *Revisioning Gender,* eds. Myra Mark Ferree, Judith Lorber, and Beth B. Hess (Thousand Oaks, Calif.: Sage Publications, 1999), 285-310.

3. Ferree, Lorber, and Hess, "Gender and Sexuality," 1999.

4. Ferree, Lorber, and Hess, "Gender and Sexuality," 1999.

5. Robin Leidner, "Serving Hamburgers and Selling Insurance: Gender, Work, and Identity in Interactive Service Jobs," *Gender & Society* 5, no. 2 (June 1991): 154-177; Kath Weston, "Production as Means, Production as Metaphor: Women's Struggles to Enter the Trades," in *Uncertain Terms: Negotiating Gender in American Culture,* eds. Faye Ginsburg and Anna Lowenhaupt Tsing (Boston: Beacon Press, 1990), 137-151.

6. Martin and Collinson, "Gender and Sexuality," 1999, 289-290.

7. Leidner, "Serving Hamburgers," 1991.

8. Ann M. Morrison, Randall P. White, and Ellen Van Velsor, "Executive Women on a Tightrope," in *The Best of Psychology Today,* 1987.

9. Findings in general, however, suggest that these characteristics are not a primary or major type of orientation women take to their jobs For a summary of articles, see Anne Statham, Eleanor M. Miller, and Hans O. Mauksch, "The Integration

Work: A Second-Order Analysis of Qualitative Research," in *The Worth of Women's Work: A Qualitative Synthesis*, eds. Anne Statham, Eleanor M. Miller, and Hans O. Mauksch (Albany: State University of New York Press, 1988): 25.

10. Martin and Collinson, "Gender and Sexuality," 1999.

11. As a cautionary note, I have no evidence that confirms or denies these perceptions. They are the respondents' beliefs about the effects of gender.

12. Arlie Hochschild, *The Managed Heart: Commercialization of Human Feeling* (Berkeley: University of California Press, 1983).

13. This last claim is contradicted by NAR data, which show that men lead in sales volume.

14. These comments indicate that male realtors construct gender in relationship to the job also, but in terms that cast women as less suitable.

15. Barbara J. Thomas and Barbara F. Reskin, "A Woman's Place is Selling Homes: Occupational Change and the Feminization of Real Estate Sales," in *Job Queues, Gender Queues: Explaining Women's Inroads into Male Occupations*, eds. Barbara F. Reskin and Patricia A. Roos (Philadelphia, Pa.: Temple University Press, 1990), 211.

## Chapter Six

# Good Job/Bad Job: The Perks and Piques of Selling Houses

> Job queues and labor queues govern labor market outcomes: employers hire workers from as high in the labor queue as possible, and workers accept the best jobs available to them. As a result the best jobs go to the most preferred workers, and less attractive jobs go to workers lower in the labor queue; bottom-ranked workers may go jobless, and the worst jobs may be left unfilled.
> —**Barbara F. Reskin** and **Patricia A. Roos,** *Job Queues, Gender Queues: Explaining Women's Inroads into Male Occupations.*[1]

> Oh, we love it! We love it! You know, commission work is a frightening thing; you do kind of have to walk the line. But I have not found anybody that does not like it. They [people who quit] got out of it because things were going kind of slow, this type of thing, but not because they did not like selling real estate.
> —**Judith Jacobs**, five years' experience selling real estate.

What do people like about their work? Aside from the monetary reward, what keeps workers going back day after day? Or what makes them decide to leave a job? How do they weigh the pros and cons of particular occupations? The focus of this chapter is the women's assessment of their work: the reasons they chose a career in real estate and the positive and negative aspects of the work as they experienced it.

People are never free from all constraints in choosing a job. They are limited by structural factors, such as their education, geographic location, family responsibilities, possibly their religious beliefs, and the least mutable variables: their race, gender, and/or their age. They are limited also by how they have been socialized—what they "know" about their abilities and their suitability for specific activities (for example, a woman may "know" that she could not operate heavy machinery because she has always heard that women cannot do that job). Finally, choices are limited by opportunity, by whether or not an employer is willing to give an individual a chance in a job. Within these limitations, however, people do have job preferences and some options in choosing their work. They exercise these options to whatever extent possible.

One theoretical explanation of how and why different categories of people end up in particular occupations is the *queuing* model. This model views workers' placement in occupational fields as the result of two processes occurring in concert: the availability of jobs and workers' motivations to fill them. Thus, workers' occupational placement is a dual-queuing process: employers and employees represent contradictory interests and differential power in shaping the composition of occupations. Employers rank workers in labor queues, hiring workers in order of the employers' preferences. Employers weigh the skills possessed by job applicants, as well as the applicants' education, age, gender, race, or whatever other characteristics the employer considers significant.

At the same time, workers rank jobs into job queues, accepting whatever jobs are available in order of desirability. The desirability of a job depends on objective working conditions, including salary level, job title, workload, work hours, responsibilities, and possibilities for advancement. Desirability also includes subjective factors, such as intrinsic satisfaction with a job, the prestige of the job, and the compatibility of the job with one's other obligations.

Barbara F. Reskin and Patricia A. Roos employed the queuing model to analyze a dozen occupations, including real estate, that became disproportionately more female during the 1970s. They focused on labor queuing, particularly the process of occupational feminization—the forces that make occupations more accessible to women. Reskin and Roos emphasized changes in employers' preferences, contending that there is less need to explain how workers rank jobs, because "readers, as past, present, and future workers, already understand this process."[2] While this is perhaps true on an intuitive level, it is insightful to hear how workers interpret their own decisions, to understand the meanings that workers give to their initial attraction and continuing preference for an occupation. Consequently, my interest is job queues—the factors that determine how workers rank their job preferences. In keeping with the metaphor of a framework (see Introduction), I am looking at how the characteristics of this occupation influence the design of workers' lives.

Autonomy and control in the work setting are important determinants of job attractiveness and satisfaction for workers in a wide variety of occupations, from domestic service to high-level administration.[3] Autonomy includes being able to determine the content of one's work, setting one's own standards, and controlling the pace and routine of the work. These qualities seem to have greater impact on workers' feelings of accomplishment and worth, dignity and self-motivation than do traditional standards of professional status and prestige.[4]

Another determinant of the desirability of a job is the amount of emotion work it includes. Emotional labor can give workers satisfaction in doing "good work" by helping others.[5]

Changes in the structural properties of queues—the order and size of jobs and workers available at any particular time—and in the intensity of preferences by employers and workers redistribute groups of workers across occupations. Workers become more desirable to employers in periods of labor shortages. This could be a general labor shortage, as during a period of economic expansion when unemployment rates are low and opportunities for work are numerous, or it could be a shortage of a formerly preferred category of worker, as other jobs attract those workers away from a formerly desirable occupation. As groups of workers move up in the labor queue, that is, as they become more desirable to employers, the jobs that they abandon are passed to the next group in the queue. Labor queues tend also to be gender queues, since employers usually rank women and men differently in terms of potential productivity and labor costs. I presented historical examples of the successive movement of queues in chapter 1.

Recent findings indicate that in general, women and men workers rank occupations on the basis of the same criteria.[6] Although family-related issues are often cited in explaining women's work aspirations and attitudes, job-related issues such as working conditions, income, prestige, interesting work, job security, policies of recruitment and promotion are equally important influences on women's responses to work opportunities. Women move into occupations that have been dominated by men when the opportunity arises, simply because in general those occupations are preferable to most traditionally female occupations. In particular, the earnings potential for these jobs is higher than for female workers as a group, and the desire for high wages is a primary selection factor for women as well as men.[7]

In addition, women with families may choose specific occupations that they perceive as compatible with their domestic obligations. This type of compatibility is based on features such as flexible hours, innovative scheduling, on-site child care, and job-sharing. As another factor, emotion work *may* be more important to women than to men: perhaps women make a resource out of their capacity to manage feelings and relate to others.[8]

There are interesting parallels between workers' preferences for work in direct selling organizations (DSOs), such as Tupperware and Mary Kay Cosmetics, and real estate sales work. Both types of occupations are contingent forms of interactive service work.[9] Attractive features of DSOs include a sense of control over work, a belief in unlimited income potential, the ability to fit work around family obligations, and workers' limited alternatives—other available jobs are lower paying, dull and routine, with little opportunity for advancement. The structure of DSO work gives salespeople a sense that their work is meaningful, that they are providing an important service to their customers.[10]

Residential real estate has ranked high on the job queue for women since at least the 1950s. The women in this study identified several reasons for this high ranking. They also described the negative characteristics of the job.

## The Perquisites: Positive Features of the Work

> I think you really get high when you sell somebody exactly what they want. It's really a good feeling. And I have a way of putting myself in their shoes. I think that's important, to know what they want, where they want to be, and then to help them find it.
> —**Erika Stewart**, fourteen years' experience selling real estate.

As with workers in other fields, the women in this study focused on job-related issues in describing why they had entered the field and what they found appealing about it. They were, on the whole, very satisfied with their jobs. Previous studies suggest that women perceive residential real estate sales as an occupation that will allow them easy entry with low educational requirements, flexible working hours, autonomy, high income, and opportunities for self-employment.[11] I expected that my respondents would have chosen to enter the field for similar reasons, but that they would have found contradictions in their actual experiences. As discussed in chapter 4, these contradictions did occur, particularly as the need to work long hours meant that the job did not allow as much flexibility as they had anticipated. I was interested in what characteristics compensated for the contradictions and made the job continue to be attractive for women who stayed in it.

The respondents cited flexibility as the most common reason for choosing real estate sales, followed by the potential for high earnings, autonomy, and the relatively low entry requirements. Many also listed compatibility with family obligations as important, seeing this compatibility as a function of the above job characteristics.

Prior to entering the real estate field, the interviewees had held a range of jobs in relatively low-paying, high-stress fields, including clerical, teaching, social work, and other sales. Compared to these experiences, real estate was higher paying and offered greater autonomy and satisfaction.

This sense of relative improvement came up repeatedly in the interviews, and for women coming from these occupations, greater income potential was the most significant factor in their attraction to real estate. For others, who had been making fairly good wages previously, the ability to set their own hours and otherwise gain greater autonomy were more important. The flexibility of real estate sales work allows its practitioners to interweave family-related tasks with their paid work more easily than do other types of work that occupy a fixed set of hours of every day.

For most of the women, who had at least some college education, real estate was appealing primarily because they anticipated that it would allow them greater autonomy than would their other occupational options to pursue outside interests and obligations while earning a good income. For example, Deborah Engels had been a schoolteacher and switched to real estate for the following reasons:

> The flexible hours . . . thinking that I'd be able to play tennis and do some other things that I wanted to do during the day. In teaching I got really tired of being stuck in a classroom from eight [o'clock] in the morning until three-thirty.

At the time she entered the field, Deborah had a preschool-age child, and she also liked the fact that she could do most of her office work at home (see chapter 4). For women without college degrees, the perceived flexibility and high income potential were still paramount, but they combined these with the low entry requirements of the field. Tonia Marks, who had been a full-time mother and had never held a paying job prior to entering the real estate field, gave the following explanation:

> Without a college education, I found myself limited in what I could do that would have income potential, let alone flexibility. Real estate did not require college, gave me unlimited income potential depending on how hard I elected to work, allowed me to be my own boss while I could juggle my schedule around my family and basically take control of myself.

Tonia's narrative includes all of the most common attractions: one can become a realtor without obtaining a college degree; one can earn as much money as desired; the job provides autonomy and flexibility.

When flexibility was considered in a broader sense than just being able to set one's own working hours, it included flexibility in income-earning potential. Many of the women realtors stated that "the sky is the limit" as far as earning potential, and believed that their income was limited only by how much they were willing to work. Ironically, the two types of flexibility—of scheduling and income—are often mutually exclusive. Because one's income depends on hard work,[12] long hours reduce one's free time to do other things. Chris Harden contended that a widespread misconception propelled many people into this occupation:

> The overwhelming majority want to make over seventy-five thousand dollars a year and they want to work less than forty hours a week. They think there's a magic formula for how to do that. There is no magic formula. At some point you either choose, I'm going to take the easy route and no income, or little income, or I'm going to work myself to death and have a good income. So there are bound to be more profitable professions, where you make the big bucks and don't work the same hours that we do.

The women recognized that they had to make a trade-off between maximizing their business opportunities and reserving times when they could be "off duty." Inez Evans, who had been selling for eleven years, beginning when her three children were very young, said that she had learned gradually to maximize the advantages of flexibility:

> In the sense that I can schedule my home time and my time away from home [the work is flexible]. Like in the summer, every Wednesday we [her family] go out on the boat. And I've had my [occasional] weekend that I take off. I allow more time. I go to all the kids' games. I find that I can control my time better now. . . . Once I learned that I had to say I had another appointment or commitment, then I could block off time.

Through experience, the women learned how to have both types of flexibility. And in spite of these limitations, most of the women still found flexibility to be a primary attraction. The desire for flexible scheduling is at least partly gender-related. Although men may also appreciate this sort of freedom, women are more often seeking ways to integrate the obligations of paid and family work.

Tonia Mark's desire to take control of her work (see quotation above) was articulated by others as one of the advantages of being self-employed: not having to work for someone else. For example, Colleen Ewing had resigned from her job in a social service agency because she did not get along with her supervisor:

> At that point in time, I thought the nicest thing about real estate would be if I didn't like somebody, I just wouldn't have to work for them! I wouldn't have to worry about it!

Of course, in reality realtors often find themselves working with difficult clients (as is discussed later in this chapter) and/or broker/managers. In a sense too, they are working for the broker/manager of their firm. But Colleen felt much less constrained by these possibilities because in real estate sales work she had the option of dropping customers if they proved too incompatible, and to change companies if she did not feel comfortable with her colleagues.

The women had found several other features of the job that pleased them: They liked the excitement and unpredictability of their day-to-day experiences. They found the job challenging and were proud of their abilities to meet those challenges. They liked seeing and showing houses. They enjoyed the sense that they were helping people find a home, and the opportunity to interact with a wide variety of people. Judith Jacobs had been selling for five years and had been attracted initially by the potential for high earnings. She had found several other aspects of the job appealing:

> Every transaction is a little bit different. I think the part that I like best is, it's a dream, and to see that face when that dream comes true, you know, when they get into the house.... I just like real estate basically because I have that personality where I like helping people. I like to make money too [laughs], but I like helping people and it gives me gratification when you get into that house.

Judith expresses the rhetoric of rewards involved. The interviewees tended to define their work as helping people and matching people with houses, and many made similar statements about "making people feel good" by selling them a house. Emotional labor can be rewarding for workers, when they are convinced that their work is providing meaningful services, as when flight attendants succeed in calming nervous passengers or insurance agents feel that they have persuaded their customers to protect themselves by buying insurance.[13]

As discussed in chapter 5, workers frequently see a relationship between their gender and their success or failure in a job. Workers who interpret their jobs as congruent with proper enactment of their gender are more likely to be satisfied with their work than are those who do not. Because of their perception that it was one of the aspects of the job that women did best, I anticipated that the emotional labor would be the most rewarding feature for women selling residential real estate, and this expectation was at least partially correct.

The realtors' self-identities were shaped in part by their interactions with their clients; and when these interactions were positive, when the customers were satisfied with their agents' efforts, the realtors felt good about themselves. There was also a "halo effect" to the work, since the realtors came into contact with lawyers, bankers, property developers, and sometimes wealthy clients, and these contacts gave them a sense of participating in the power-brokering and other privileges of class and status otherwise denied them.[14] They took pride in the skills they had developed through licensing courses and additional workshops and seminars. They dressed well and took care with their offices and cars to convey a professional appearance that enhanced their self-concept, and interacted with other realtors to reinforce positive perspectives in their work. They found honor in the autonomy of being independent contractors.

In short, the features of the job that respondents cited repeatedly as being the most attractive can be grouped together as providing autonomy, flexibility, and feelings of self-worth. The explanation of this level of job satisfaction lies in the limited alternatives available. Real estate was more flexible and promised higher earnings than any of the other jobs they could imagine for themselves. At the same time the respondents recognized that the work had significant drawbacks.

## The Piques: Drawbacks of the Work

> I think everybody I knew in real estate painted a much rosier picture of it than what it can be. There's no way anyone could begin to tell you all the different aspects you're going to run into—all the nightmares and all the sleepless hours you're going to have, trying to get a deal together. You know, this person is going to lose their house if this one doesn't close on this house, and so on. There is no way you can envision that until you're in the middle of it.
> —**Allison Foote**, three years' experience selling real estate.

Although for the most part, the women interviewed evaluated real estate sales work positively, there were several recurring themes about what they did not like in the work. These themes included issues of timing, emotion work, and the burdensome paper work that went with the job.

The emotional labor involved in selling real estate was rewarding when the realtor felt that she had helped clients find the "right" house, but it could also be a source of stress. Persuading clients to buy houses and helping them feel comfortable with their decisions meant that the realtor must separate her personal feelings from her professional demeanor, and manage the emotion-charged experiences of clients. While these efforts gave the salesperson a sense of doing "good work"[15] when she succeeded in matching a prospective buyer with a home, the work also forced the realtor to control her own feelings. For example, the salesperson might have to feign enthusiasm for a house she did not like personally, or maintain a cordial relationship with rude or demanding clients.

Elaine Bird described the kinds of situations in which she felt that emotion work got to be burdensome:

> Sometimes you just don't know what to expect. People will fly off the handle at you for the least little thing. You think, "I don't deserve this." Sometimes you'd do everything, you'd like live with them for four months.[16] You'd see every quirk they had, like if somebody died in the family, they

expected you to console them. If they had a fight with their husband, the wife would call you up and say, "He's in a really bad mood today, but I want to do such and such, so when you see him . . ." I mean, I had so much of that, it's unbelievable. Or vice versa. The husband would say, "I really can't afford this, this, and this. She wants it. When we meet today, can you do anything to talk her out of it?" And then the people would get there and get in a fight, because the wife would really want the stuff, and the husband really wouldn't. I'd be trying to talk her out of it, for whatever scientific reason I could come up with, and she'd be getting pissed off with me. But actually I was trying to do him a favor. Oh yeah, husbands and wives get in fights a lot in front of us [realtors]. There was a lot of that. And when you deal with a lot of people, sometimes you get them mixed up. You know, "Am I supposed to act like this person wants this, or doesn't want this?" There was a lot of that and it was hard.

Situations like this made selling real estate a type of "dirty work," or work that contradicts one's inner convictions of honesty, integrity, morality.[17] Many occupations include some dirty work, tasks that are physically, psychologically, or morally degrading. In real estate, the need to manipulate clients, or the knowledge that the public perception of realtors includes this element, made the salesperson feel dishonorable. Beth Tripp said that she was surprised by "the rejection" that she experienced as part of the job:

You will probably have seventy-five percent of the people talking to you reject you. If ten people walk through an open house, you'll be lucky if you get one person you can work with. That's tough, because generally I feel like I'm a likable person, and I've never had trouble making friends. [But] When you approach somebody at an open house and they go "Oh, you're a realtor" [sounds disgusted], that's tough.

In addition to generating feelings of rejection, the problems of dealing with customers who did not understand the realtors' work, or who could (and often would) take their business elsewhere at anytime, produced frustration, anger, hurt feelings, and sometimes, lower self-esteem for the sales agent. In this respect, real estate sales work shares the burden of other forms of interactive service work, involving as it does direct interaction between salespeople and their customers. This direct interaction gives the customer power to direct and sanction the worker more immediately than do situations where the client never comes into contact with the producer.[18]

Several women said that the general public did not understand what realtors do, and therefore had unrealistic expectations and demands. They described the "dishonesty" or "disloyalty" of clients, who did not reveal potential credit or other problems that would inhibit a closing, or who switched agents after weeks of working with them.[19] Kendra Jones described the volatility of clients:

> People are so emotional when it comes to a home. It's not like going in and buying a dress, or even a car for that matter. They walk into a house and they just suddenly feel "(Gasp)Oh!, this is it!" They forget that they ever had an agent. I guess I didn't realize the difficulty in keeping people loyal and keeping them under control.

When these emotions led clients to write a contract without consulting their agent, or to turn in anger against the agent if things went wrong with the process, the emotion work became one of the worst aspects of the job. Such negative reactions were hard to reconcile with a sense of doing important work.

Workers respond to the dirty aspects of their work by reinterpreting it positively or, if that cannot be done, by distancing themselves from it.[20] Thus, realtors would talk to each other, commiserating about commonly experienced frustrations, or even joking about them. Elaine Bird told me that a woman friend of hers who was also a realtor had put together a list of insiders' jokes about the work, which was "hysterical. I just laugh at all the things she's saying because they're so true.... The problems that you deal with, and the people ... it's priceless."

While flexibility was cited as one of the positive features of the work, flexibility also had its disadvantages. The women did not anticipate the long hours required, or that flexibility would be limited severely by the requirement of working evenings and weekends. Tess White, who described previously the ability to take time to make bunny cakes or take her children to the doctor, also recognized the time constraints of the job:

> Some of it was a little disappointing, because you end up actually working more than forty hours a week. You work a lot more evenings and you work three weekends a month minimum, if not four.[21]

The other major source of dissatisfaction was the extensive paperwork that accompanied the job. Paperwork included writing newspaper ads for listings, writing contracts for clients who were making an offer on a house, writing descriptions of listings, and all of the steps involved in closing a sale. Sandra Berry described some of this work:

> All day it seems like I do a lot of paperwork, following up on sales, closings, writing thank you notes to people coming to an open house, stat sheets for listings, following up on getting feedback on people who showed the listings. Things like that. A lot of people don't see the kind of work that's involved. They think all we do is go out and show houses. But I think more of my time is spent doing paperwork, meeting an appraiser, meeting a termite inspector, arranging for repairs for termite damage. I talk to contractors all the time, and get prices for roof repairs because of a home inspection. Things like that we do all the time.

When asked what about the job they would change if they could, the most common response focused on the tedium of paperwork. Several women stated that they would like to have enough money to hire a "personal assistant" to handle the administrative work such as following up on arrangements with banks, inspectors, appraisers, surveyors, closing agents, and so on. They told me that such a position was becoming more common among realtors with high volume sales records, but none of my respondents had yet reached the level where they felt they could afford to hire someone to help them. Expenses for such an assistant would be paid by the individual realtor rather than by their firms. By 1998, none of the women had acquired such an assistant, although several said that some of their colleagues had one and that the concept was more common than it had been in 1990.

For the most part, dissatisfaction with the job centered around the lack of complete control over their work: they could not control their clients' emotions or loyalty, the specific hours that they might have to work, or the amount of paperwork that had to be done. They also had no control over many of the variables that determined whether a client would actually complete the purchase of a home. Andrea Loomis, who had been selling real estate for four years, explained what she liked least about the work:

> The unpredictability. I'm always frustrated when things that I thought should work out don't work out. It's very hard; it's like an emotional roller coaster. They tell you when you're in this profession, don't ever count on it being closed until the check's in your hand, and that's so true, because it's just pitfalls all the way.

Although they appreciated the variability of the work, they felt that the unpredictability produced anxiety. Many factors could interfere with the completion of a sale. This quality of unpredictability was counter to the women's desire for autonomy and control of their working conditions, and thus a major source of dissatisfaction.

Income was a final source of dissatisfaction. Earnings were generally higher than in the respondents' previous occupations, but not usually as high as they had expected. In addition, many found that their dreams of earning high salaries were thwarted by the expenses incurred on the job. As independent contractors, salespeople were essentially self-employed and had to pay their own social security and whatever retirement plan they had, as well as advertising, transportation, professional dues and license fees, and other expenses. Yet they had to split their sales commissions with their companies (see chapter 1 for descriptions of the expenses.) Several women mentioned out-of-pocket expenses, especially for advertising, with no certainty of recouping their costs, as the most dissatisfying aspect of the work. Ellie Denton describes another unexpected expense:

> They fail to tell you about the tax situation. Never having had a job that they didn't take your taxes out, you don't really get the real meaning of the IRS until the end of the year. You've made seventy-two thousand dollars and you didn't have to pay any taxes. And the tax accountant says, "Ok, you owe these people twenty-one thousand by April 15." And you've already spent all the money. That's how second and third mortgages develop on your house! I know a lot better now. And I have my four hundred dollar penalty over there because I didn't pay it quarterly. I paid all my taxes last year but I just got a bill from the IRS saying "Here's your fine for not paying it quarterly." So now I pay it quarterly, which I still have not done. I've definitely learned my lesson.

Ellie had worked several other jobs prior to entering real estate sales work, but never as an independent contractor. Her experience mirrored that of many of the other respondents after their first year, when they discovered the grim costs of not paying their income taxes on their own. And once they had learned that lesson, they still had to go through the recurring hassle of keeping up with their tax-related expenses and filing their quarterly payments on time.

In spite of these complaints about the costs of being independent contractors, desired changes were not suggested in terms of the contingent nature of their work. Only one of the respondents, a single mother, mentioned the lack of employer-provided benefits as a concern: "The scariest thing about this job is that when you stop, you have no benefits."[22] The other respondents seemed to feel that the rewards of independence outweighed the costs.

## Weighing the Pros and Cons of the Work

In summary, selling real estate has its merits and its flaws, and some of the determination of which features are evaluated as positive and which as negative depends on the individual situations, such as the stage in the life cycle or the personal preferences of the women who are making the assessment. Other assessments are influenced by outside events such as the economy, so that when the housing market is booming the unpredictability is exciting, never knowing how high one's sales might go. When the market flattens out, realtors do not know if they will be able to pay their bills that month.

In general, the negative features of the job relate to exploitations of time and emotions, although the women did not articulate their frustrations in these terms. In fact, their rhetoric reflects the alienation of much interactive service work, in which the workers believe that they are performing meaningful services for their clients and overlook the ways that their labor enhances the profits of their employers.[23]

There is a high turnover rate for residential salespeople. My respondents estimated that at least fifty percent of women who entered real estate dropped out within the first two years. The respondents thought that the principal reason that people had for leaving the occupation was finding that they could not make as much money as they expected and/or as they needed to make. Other reasons that respondents cited for leaving the field included finding the demands of the job incompatible with their own preferences and/or their other obligations, and deciding that another occupation was more attractive. Since I did not interview women who had left the field, I have focused on what factors provided satisfaction and caused frustration for experienced salespeople who planned to stay in the occupation.

Overall, this study supports the findings of other research on the factors that attract workers to certain occupations and what characteristics explain their retention or defection. In addition, the analysis adds to the literature by providing detailed descriptions of workers' feelings about their work and the contradictions embedded in their positive and negative evaluations. As with many occupations, people are more satisfied if they feel that they chose their work and can control their working conditions.

# Notes

1. Barbara F. Reskin and Patricia A. Roos, *Job Queues, Gender Queues: Explaining Women's Inroads into Male Occupations* (Philadelphia, Pa.: Temple University Press, 1990), 38.

2. Reskin and Roos, *Job Queues, Gender Queues*, 1990.

3. See, for example, Sheila K. Collins, "Women at the Top of Women's Fields: Social Work, Nursing, and Education," in *The Worth of Women's Work: A Qualitative Synthesis*, eds. Anne Statham, Eleanor M. Miller, and Hans O. Mauksch (New York: State University of New York Press, 1988), 187-201, and Mary Romero, *Maid in the U.S.A.* (New York: Routledge, Chapman, and Hall, 1992).

4. Anne Statham, Eleanor M. Miller, and Hans O. Mauksch, "The Integration Work: A Second-Order Analysis of Qualitative Research," in *The Worth of Women's Work* eds. Statham, Miller, and Mauksch, 34.

5. Jane C. Hood, "The Caretakers: Keeping the Area up and the Family Together," in *The Worth of Women's Work*, eds. Statham, Miller, and Mauksch, 93-107.

6. Roslyn L. Feldberg and Evelyn N. Glenn, "Male and Female: Job versus Gender Models in the Sociology of Work," in *Women and Work: Problems and Perspectives*, eds. Rachel Kahn Hut, Arlene Kaplan Daniels, and Richard Colvard (New York: Oxford University Press, 1982), 65-80; Christopher Jencks, Larry Perman, and Lee Rainwater, "What is a Good Job? A New Measure of Labor-Market Success," *American Journal of Sociology* 93, no. 6 (May 1988): 1322-1357.

7. Irene Padavic, "White Collar Work Values and Women's Interest in Blue-Collar Jobs," *Gender & Society* 6, no. 2 (June 1992): 215-230; Reskin and Roos, *Job Queues, Gender Queues*, 1990.

8. This is Hochschild's contention in Arlie Hochschild, *The Managed Heart: Commercialization of Human Feeling* (Berkeley: University of California Press, 1983).

9. Nicole W. Biggart, *Charismatic Capitalism: Direct Selling Organizations in America* (Chicago: University of Chicago Press, 1989), 50, classifies both the Mary Kay and Tupperware sales forces as women "of modest education and few credentials in families of middling income."

10. Biggart, *Charismatic Capitalism,* 1989; Maureen Connelly and Patricia

Rhoton, "Women in Direct Sales: A Comparison of Mary Kay and Amway Sales Workers," in *The Worth of Women's Work,* edss. Statham, Miller, and Mauksch, 1988, 245-264; Robin Leidner, "Serving Hamburgers and Selling Insurance: Gender, Work, and Identity in Interactive Service Jobs," *Gender & Society* 5, no. 2 (June 1991): 154-177.

11. J. D. House, *Contemporary Entrepreneurs: The Sociology of Residential Real Estate Agents* (Westport, Conn.: Greenwood Press, 1977); Barbara J. Thomas and Barbara F. Reskin, "A Woman's Place is Selling Homes: Occupational Change Dand the Feminization of Real Estate Sales," in *Job Queues, Gender Queues: Explaining Women's Inroads into Male Occupations,* eds. Barbara F. Reskin and Patricia A. Roos (Philadelphia, Pa.: Temple University Press, 1990), 205-223.

12. In part, at least, although most of the interviewees believed it depended entirely on hard work, that their income was limited only by their own ambition (see the discussion with Beth Tripp, chapter 1).

13. Hochschild, *The Managed Heart,* 1983; Leidner, "Serving Hamburgers," 1991.

14. I am grateful to C. Ray Wingrove for this insight (personal communication).

15. Hood, "The Caretakers," 1988.

16. This respondent was working in new construction, with custom built homes. Thus, she worked with clients from the time they chose a site until their house was complete.

17. Everett C. Hughes, "Work and Self," in *The Sociological Eye: Selected Papers on Work, Self, & the Study of Society,* ed. Everett C. Hughes (Chicago: Aldine-Atherton, 1951, 1971; Hannah Meara, "Honor in Dirty Work: The Case of American Meat Cutters and Turkish Butchers," *Sociology of Work and Occupations* 1, no. 3 (August 1974): 259-283.

18. Howard Becker (*Outsiders: Studies in the Sociology of Deviance* [New York: Free Press, 1963], 82) describes this dilemma:
> The service occupations are, in general, distinguished by the fact that the worker in them comes into more or less direct contact and personal contact with the ultimate consumer of the product of his work, the client for whom he performs the service. Consequently, the client is able to direct or attempt to direct the worker at his task and to apply sanctions of various kinds, ranging from informal pressure to the withdrawal of his patronage and the conferring of it on some others of the many people who perform the service.

19. House (*Contemporary Entrepreneurs,* 1977, 69) describes additional sources of conflict in relations between agents and clients, and characterizes such relations as examples of "imbalanced reciprocity, agents having to assert themselves continually to maintain their clients' loyalty."

20. Leidner, "Serving Hamburgers," 1991.

21. As discussed in chapter 3, not everyone worked these hours, but the point is

still important: the work was more demanding than many had anticipated.

22. This prospect would, of course, be especially frightening for women who were the sole breadwinners in their families.

23. See, for example, Biggart, *Charismatic Capitalism,* 1989, Connelly and Rhoton, "Women in Direct Sales," 1988; Jane C. Hood, "The Caretakers," 1988; Robin Leidner, "Serving Hamburgers," 1991.

# Conclusion

Imagining worlds yet to come is not done by gazing into crystal balls, of course, but by sorting through trends evident in the present and identifying the ones most likely to gain momentum in the years to come.
—**Kai Erikson**, *The Nature of Work: Sociological Perspectives*[1]

My real estate image was there was a realtor when I was growing up who was very successful. I come from a very middle-class environment. And she had a big car, and a nicer house than we did, and she seemed very independent, self-sufficient, had a good sense of humor, and everybody knew her. And I guess when I thought about real estate I thought about her.
—**Beth Tripp**, three years' experience selling real estate.

This final chapter looks back over the basic characteristics of the job of selling residential real estate, and at how this occupation illustrates the nature of work for a growing proportion of the contemporary workforce. The framework of working conditions and family characteristics determines the pattern by which people weave their many obligations and activities into a lifestyle. Whether that weaving consists of many overlapping shades or of distinct blocks depends on how permeable the boundaries are between the realms of work and family, as determined by the structures of the job and family and by the preferences of the individuals. Gender plays a role in how the framework shapes the final production.

Realtors are independent contractors who affiliate themselves with specific companies but move about frequently. They receive few benefits and must pay for their own health insurance, social security, and retirement plans. They are responsible for paying their income taxes on a regular basis and know that their income depends entirely on the sales commissions they can generate.

Realtors set their own working hours, and can take time off from work whenever they choose. However, they need to work regularly and steadily to establish themselves in the business and to achieve a satisfactory sales volume. Workdays include time driving clients to view houses, making phone calls, and doing paperwork. The work requires large amounts of time and attention, arranged for the convenience of clients, not of families. This is especially true in the first few years of getting established in the business, although to be successful, the work will always be labor intensive, since customers demand a great deal of individual attention from realtors.

The boundaries between work and home are relatively flexible, since realtors go back and forth between the two realms. This sort of flexibility is an important characteristic of jobs that provide a compatible framework for weaving together work and family obligations. Realtors may have appointments to show houses at four o'clock in the afternoon and seven-thirty at night, and use the time between the two appointments to fix dinner, supervise children's homework, and make phone calls for a school bake sale. The personal preferences of the individual for more or less permeable boundaries will influence how much more the two realms overlap. She might make business-related phone calls during the meal preparation, and keep her cellular phone on for calls from her children while she is showing a house. Or she might not do either of these things, believing that her personal and business lives should be as separated as possible. In addition to her personal perspective on the boundary issue, her decision will be influenced by her family composition. If she has young children she is more likely to breach the boundaries; if her children are old enough to be on their own more, and/or she has a spouse who shares the parenting and housework equally, she may be able to maintain a more rigid boundary between home and work.

Regardless of the different perspectives on the boundary between work and home, working hours must be compatible with the needs of prospective clients, which means that for most salespeople, at least some evenings and weekends must be spent showing homes, making listing presentations, writing contracts, and so on. As a result, most realtors work longer hours than would an hourly-wage, assembly line or salaried office worker, and they are likely to work some evenings and weekends. While they may feel that they are never completely "free" of work obligations, they also appreciate the privilege of being able to arrange their workdays as they prefer, working where and when it suits them and their clients. As a result, however, the work has the potential for being all-encompassing. The pull of the work is seductive, and the more success they experience, the more temptation there is to work longer and longer. As Arlie Hochschild has argued in *The Time Bind*, when workers find themselves recognized and appreciated more for their paid work than for their family work, they are likely to spend increasing amounts of time on the job. Many of the respondents stated or implied that they would work longer hours, would allow themselves to become "obsessed" with their careers in real estate if they did not have family obligations.

Another characteristic of this occupation is that it represents a particular type of interactive service work, which requires a high degree of emotional labor. In this type of work, the interaction between the worker and the customer is crucial to the worker's success in the job. Thus, in real estate sales work, the realtor must establish and maintain a positive relationship with the client. Realtors must persuade their customers to trust them as they participate together in finding a house and negotiating its purchase. The process is an emotionally charged one for the customer, who often has no direct contact with any of the other parties involved in the sale of a house but has frequent contact with the realtor.

At the same time as s/he must handle the emotions of a client, the realtor must also manage her/his own emotions, always presenting a positive façade. The realtor/client relationship must include loyalty to the realtor or the client will engage another agent or act on his/her own in negotiating a home sale or purchase, and the realtor will not collect a commission.

Realtors refer to themselves as professionals, and strive to win greater respect from the general public. While the occupation does not include all of the characteristics of a profession, it seems appropriate to conclude that it is involved in a process of professionalization. This process includes moving from part-time to full-time work, requiring formal training and credentials, and having a national organization that will create a code of ethics and work to achieve legal recognition of the occupation as a profession. While most realtors practicing today have not attended a college-accredited training program, many believe that such credentials will become necessary in the near future. Licensing already requires the completion of training approved by a state board.

Being classified as professionals is important to realtors' self-perception. They talk about behaving "professionally." They want the public to perceive them as responsible professionals, and they maintain a professional appearance in their demeanor and in the ways that they conduct their work. Such a designation influences how much respect outsiders accord to workers in a particular field. Professionalization may increase the amount of compensation that an occupation is able to command. In the case of independent contractors, professionalization makes their commissions more palatable to their clients. The professional can command large hourly fees on the basis of specialized knowledge, in the same manner as attorneys or physicians, for example.

For realtors, as for workers in many fields, gender expectations and family responsibilities intersect with one's work experiences. The time commitment and adaptations in the arrangements for household labor are more demanding than the women who participated in this study had anticipated when they started selling houses. Like most women with paid work and families, the realtors often find themselves coming home at night and folding laundry, or making business phone calls while they prepare dinner and supervise children's activities. But because they can arrange their work schedules to attend school meetings or extracurricular events with their children, or schedule doctors' appointments during the day, the job is more compatible with family responsibilities than are jobs with rigidly scheduled working hours.

The desire for a flexible schedule relates to the worker's other obligations. These obligations may be gender-related, although not gender-specific. In other words, women are likely to desire work schedules that complement their family responsibilities as fully as possible, but such preferences are not limited to women. A sample of men in residential real estate sales with similar family compositions could be compared with these women to learn how men balance their paid and unpaid work. No conclusions can be made without such a study. However, based on studies of women and men in other occupations, it is probable that men in real estate sales work do not experience the same kinds of conflicts as the women.[2] None of the respondents had full-time househusbands; most described household divisions of labor in which they, the wives, carried more than half of the workload and most of the managerial responsibility for the housework and child care. Thus, it seems reasonable to conclude that the arrangements described here for combining careers and families are gender-related. Specifically, they are women's ways of doing both kinds of work.

Other aspects of the work are tied to gender also. Although real estate salespeople include high percentages of both women and men, making this field apparently gender neutral, the women cite various job attributes that they perceive as related to gender. They explain their own successes as at least partially due to the fact that they are women, and they see both positive and negative effects of gender. The relevance of gender is a result of interactions between societal expectations and individual interpretations. The realtors enact gender in the ways they do their work, and believe that their identity as women influences their job performance as real estate agents.

The positive aspects of gender relate to two issues: the belief that customers prefer women as sales agents, and the women's own conviction that they are better than men at selling residential real estate. Both of these reasons are based on the women's selection of job characteristics that they define as compatible with their proper enactment of gender. Thus, they stress the importance of empathizing with customers, understanding families' housing needs as crucial to success in this field, and they believe that women are more likely to excel in both skills.

The women identify several attributes that they see as associated with successful real estate sales work, and that they believe to be more characteristic of women than of men. They assume that women are more emotional, intuitive, detail-oriented, sensitive, and patient than men. Women are better able to handle stress, better able to relate to women (who are, supposedly, the principal decision makers in family home buying), more empathetic than men. Respondents believe that these traits enhance one's ability to sell houses.

Those women who feel that gender has a negative effect on their work agree that gender-based differences give women an advantage in satisfying the job requirements, but feel that customers and male realtors block, or try to block, women from successfully accomplishing their tasks. In response to these prejudices, women de-emphasize gender and focus on their technical knowledge of houses and their professionalism in business dealings. Thus, they demonstrate the complex and contradictory nature of gender construction. It is a lifelong process that changes constantly as individuals interact in different settings. While individuals do not have total control over how their gender is perceived, they do have an active role in how they interpret society's expectations.

In the 1980s the trend of increasing numbers of women entering the residential sales field appeared to foreshadow a process of resegregation, in which this occupation would gradually become a woman's job. However, in the 1990s the proportion of women to men declined and then stabilized, so that by 2000 women made up fifty-eight percent of residential sales people and men made up forty-two percent. The work remains an attractive choice for men as well as women, which gives the field the potential of being a truly gender-integrated occupation. To paraphrase Barbara F. Reskin and Patricia A. Roos, in their book *Job Queues, Gender Queues*, genuine integration will occur if women and men move from gender separation to gender togetherness and if in the process, women achieve true personal and group autonomy.[3]

The data presented here give examples of women and men working together, although the women at least still see gender as a significant attribute that affects their work. Whether that perception continues or realtors gradually come to believe that gender is irrelevant to being a good realtor remains to be seen. As for the second criterion for integration, women in residential sales have achieved autonomy.

I have used the term "choice" throughout this book in referring to how the respondents became realtors. The occupation does have a preferential position for workers on their job queues. But I believe that it is misleading to overemphasize the amount of choice that workers have in their job selection. As with workers in many fields, women often find themselves selling real estate as a result of "occupational drift"[4] more than free choice. That is, they happen upon the job as an attractive possibility, rather than selecting it as an occupational goal for which they prepare themselves through a long period of training. Needing or wanting to work, they envision no alternatives that would provide comparable independence and income. However, because they see their work as a profession, women in real estate are more likely than many other workers to select their occupation because it represents a long-term career goal, as well as because it is expedient.

Objectively, there is a great potential for exploitation in this type of work, yet subjectively, the women experience it as fulfilling. The reasons for their job satisfaction are instructive in assessing what features could attract workers to similar fields, which are expected to continue growing rapidly in the next several years. The women chose real estate because of their desire to find work that would give them as much control over their working conditions as possible, and because of their perceptions that their career options were limited by their education and/or their previous job experiences. They needed and/or wanted to work, but they also needed to feel that the job they chose would be rewarding and would permit them to be independent. Real estate sales work seemed to promise these features.

One insight of this study has contradicted previous research on job selection, which has failed to recognize the significance of the *perception* of occupational choice in job satisfaction. The women in real estate sales work overlook the exploitative nature of contingent work, which includes having to pay their own social security, having no medical or vacation benefits, no retirement plan. Instead, they focus on the autonomy of the job and the feeling of doing good work that they experience. They are enabled to do so by factors in their individual situations that separate them from many contingent workers. First, many of the women are living in dual-earner families in which another worker provides a steady income, health care, and other benefits. In addition, or instead, the realtors themselves are earning a sufficiently high income to feel that they can compensate themselves for lack of benefits and weather the vagaries of commission-based incomes.

It is my conclusion that, while the women express their reasons for choosing real estate as an occupation in terms of objective factors—flexibility, autonomy, high earnings—subjective factors involving emotional labor and self-esteem are equally important in making this type of work satisfactory. The women's ability to frame their work in terms of appropriate gender enactment is a further source of satisfaction.

In looking at women who sell residential real estate, this study provides insights into how middle-class white-collar service work is evolving at the end of the twentieth century. Workers in this type of occupation represent a rapidly growing segment of the labor force, and value the relative autonomy afforded by the work. As is obvious from this and other studies of work and society, people are never simply workers, or parents, or spouses. They are women or men with different levels of education, from different races and socioeconomic backgrounds, at different stages in their lives, and different interests and needs. Their work experiences must take into account how all of these factors interact to produce the particular product, the *weaving* as Anita Ilta Garey calls it, that is a person's life.

As noted in chapter 1, the workplace has changed dramatically in the last quarter of the twentieth century, and the most significant changes have occurred in the area of employer/employee relationships. Employers rely increasingly on short-term workers, or those with whom they can negotiate short-term contracts, in order to gain flexibility in response to fluctuations in supply and demand. Employees become less committed to individual jobs, and even to particular occupations, learning that they must remain willing to shift jobs as labor markets change. One result of these changes is that workers are less likely to receive regular salaries and job-related benefits. Instead, as a floating workforce, their compensation fluctuates and they often find themselves without benefits unless they purchase such benefits themselves. Job security becomes a thing of the past. The field of real estate sales work is an example of these shifts, and the women described in this book are examples of this type of worker.

# Note

1. Kai Erikson, "Introduction," in *The Nature of Work: Sociological Perspectives,* eds. Kai Erikson and Steven P. Vallas (New Haven, Conn.: Yale University Press, 1990), 12.

2. Sarah F. Berk, "Women's Unpaid Labor: Home and Community," in *Women Working: Theories and Facts in Perspective*, 2nd edition, eds. Ann Helton Stromberg and Shirley Harkess (Mountain View, Calif.: Mayfield, 1988), 287-301; Jeanne M. Brett and Sara Yogev, "Restructuring Work for Family: How Dual-Earner Couples with Children Manage," in *Work and Family: Theory, Research, and Applications*, ed. Elizabeth B. Goldsmith (Newbury Park, Calif.: Sage Publications, 1989), 159-174; Toni M. Calasanti and Carol A. Bailey, "Gender Inequality and the Division of Household Labor in the United States and Sweden: A Socialist-Feminist Approach," *Social Problems* 38, no. 1 (February 1991): 34-53; Arlie Hochschild, *The Second Shift: Working Parents and the Revolution at Home* (New York: Viking Press, 1989); Arlie Hochschild, *The Time Bind: When Work Becomes Home and Home Becomes Work* (New York: Metropolitan Books, 1997).

3. Barbara F. Reskin and Patricia A. Roos, *Job Queues, Gender Queues: Explaining Women's Inroads into Male Occupations* (Philadelphia, Pa.: Temple University Press. 1990), 70.

4. Maureen Connelly and Patricia Rhoton, "Women in Direct Sales: A Comparison of Mary Kay and Amway Sales Workers," in *The Worth of Women's Work: A Qualitative Synthesis*, eds. Anne Statham, Eleanor M. Miller, and Hans O. Mauksch. (New York: State University of New York Press, 1988), 245-264.

# Appendix

## Table 1: Selected Characteristics of Respondents at Time of Initial Interview

|  | Number | Percentage[1] |
|---|---|---|
| **Age distribution** | | |
| 26-30 years | 2 | 7 |
| 31-35 years | 3 | 10 |
| 36-40 years | 13 | 43 |
| 41-45 years | 10 | 33 |
| 46-50 years | 2 | 7 |
| *Total* | 30 | 100 |
| **Marital status** | | |
| Never married | 1 | 3 |
| Married | 24 | 80 |
| Separated/divorced | 5 | 17 |
| *Total* | 30 | 100 |
| **Race** | | |
| White | 25 | 83 |
| African American | 5 | 17 |
| *Total* | 30 | 100 |

Continued on next page

## Table 1—continued

|  | Number | Percentage |
|---|---|---|
| **Number of children** | | |
| 0 | 1 | 3 |
| 1 | 11 | 37 |
| 2 | 13 | 43 |
| 3 | 2 | 7 |
| 4 | 1 | 3 |
| 5 | 2 | 7 |
| *Total* | 30 | 100 |
| **Age of youngest child** | | |
| 0-4 (preschool) | 9 | 31 |
| 5-12 | 14 | 48 |
| 13-17 | 3 | 10 |
| 18 or older | 3 | 10 |
| *Total* | 30 | 99 |
| **Education** | | |
| High school | 2 | 7 |
| 1-3 years of college | 13 | 43 |
| College graduate | 10 | 33 |
| Postgraduate degree | 5 | 17 |
| *Total* | 30 | 100 |
| **Previous occupation** | | |
| Clerical/lower management | 8 | 27 |
| Teaching | 7 | 23 |
| Sales | 3 | 10 |
| Social services | 3 | 10 |
| Full-time homemaking | 9 | 30 |
| *Total* | 30 | 100 |
| **Years in real estate sales** | | |
| Less than 1 | 0 | 0 |
| 1-2 | 2 | 7 |
| 3-4 | 8 | 27 |
| 5-6 | 14 | 47 |
| 7-8 | 3 | 10 |
| 9-10 | 1 | 3 |
| 10 or more | 2 | 7 |
| *Total* | 30 | 100 |

1. Percentages do not always add to 100 because of rounding.

# Interview Schedule

## Original Interviews, Spring 1990[1]

### Demographic Data

1. What is your age?

2. What is the highest year of education you have completed?

3. What is your marital status?

    a. (if married) What is your husband's occupation?

4. Do you have any children?

    a. (if yes) How many children do you have?

    b. What are your children's ages?

### Current Occupational Position, Training, Experience

5. Please describe your present position:

    a. What is your occupational title?

    b. What real estate license(s) do you hold?

6. What training did you have to get your license(s)?

7. Have you taken any additional courses/seminars since the initial licensing?

8. In what type of real estate sales do you specialize?

9. Have you handled any other specialties in the past?

10. How is your salary/commission determined?

    a. What sorts of expenses do you pay out of pocket?

    b. What does your broker/manager provide for his/her share of the sales commission?

11. Please describe your company:

    a. Is your firm locally owned or part of a national franchise?

    b. How many salespersons are associated with your firm/office?

    c. How many of these salespersons are women?

12. How long have you been affiliated with this company?

13. Were you involved in real estate sales prior to taking this position?
(if yes) For how long and in what capacity?

14. How did you become affiliated with your present company?

15. What were you doing before you started selling real estate?

16. What attracted you to real estate?

17. Before going into this occupation, did you know anyone who sold real estate?

18. What "image" or expectations did you have of real estate sales and salespeople before you entered the field yourself? How closely have your experiences matched your expectations?

19. How many homes did you sell last year?

    a. How many have you sold in the past three months.

    b. What is the average number of homes you have sold per year since you started selling real estate?

20. Do you spend a greater proportion of your time trying to find houses for customers or obtaining and selling your own listings?

21. How do you go about finding customers/clients?

## Experiencing Work

22. About how many hours do you work per week? Do you consider yourself to be working full-time or part-time?

23. Please describe a typical working day for you (what time do you start work, what do you do from hour to hour, when do you usually finish each day/evening, how is the day broken up into work and personal times?)

24. How much flexibility in working hours do you have (do you feel that you have the option of not working evenings/weekends/other times when personal or family obligations are heavy?)

25. How do you balance work and family obligations (how do you handle child care, particularly in the evenings and/or on weekends, when you are working? What about during the summers?)

26. (If married) Does your spouse provide any support that makes it possible/easier for you to work (not only financial, but emotional, practical—housework, child care, etc.)?

27. Do you have any other type of regular support—mother, mother-in-law, housekeeper, baby-sitter?

28. Some people have suggested that women can rely on their husbands' income during slack sales periods. Do you feel that this is true in your case?

    a. How do you think women and men without such support handle slack periods in real estate?

    b. In your own firm, is anyone the sole support of his/her family (either as a single parent or with a nonincome-earning spouse)? How do they manage, do you think?

29. What do you like best about your work?

30. What do you like least about it (what are the chief drawbacks/frustrations)?

31. What single change would you make in your work if you had the power to change anything?

32. Do you perceive that being a woman has affected your work opportunities in any way, either positively or negatively?

    a. How do you think women's and men's experiences in real estate sales occupations differ, if at all?

    b. Have you ever felt any resentment by male realtors toward yourself or women realtors in general?

c. Have you noticed any differences in customers' attitudes toward men and women realtors? (if yes) Have these attitudes changed in recent years?

d. Women tend to be concentrated in residential real estate rather than commercial. Do have any ideas why?

33. Do you perceive that family obligations have affected your work in any way?

34. Do you perceive that your race has affected your work in any way?

## Miscellaneous

35. Do you belong to the Women's Council of Realtors?

   a. (if yes) Why did you join the WCR?
   b. (if no) Why not?
   c. (if yes) What do you get out of belonging to the WCR?

36. What impact, if any, has the women's movement had on your work? On women's careers in real estate in general?

37. Do you have any other thoughts about the role of women in real estate sales occupations?

# Notes

1. I gratefully acknowledge the following sources for many of the questions in this schedule:
   Barbara J. Thomas and Barbara F. Reskin, "Interview Schedule for Real Estate Sales Occupations," draft: July 26, 1986. Received by personal communication.
   Ruth A. Wallace, "Catholic Women and the Creation of a New Social Reality," *Gender & Society* 2, no. 1 (March 1988): 24-38.

# Selected Bibliography

Abbott, Andrew. "The Sociology of Work and Occupations." *Annual Review of Sociology*, vol. 19 (1993): 187-209.

Acker, Joan. "Forward." Pp. ix-xi in *Gendered Practices in Working Life*, edited by Liisa Rantalaiho and Tuula Heiskanen. New York: St. Martin's Press, 1997.

Aronson, Jane. "Women's Sense of Responsibility for the Care of Old People: But Who Else is Going to Do It?" *Gender & Society* 6, no.1 (March 1992): 8-29.

Auster, Carol J. *The Sociology of Work: Concepts and Cases*. Thousand Oaks, Calif.: Pine Forge Press, 1996.

Beach, Betty. *Integrating Work and Family Life*. New York: State University of New York Press, 1989.

Becker, Howard S. *Outsiders: Studies in the Sociology of Deviance*. New York: The Free Press, 1963.

Berk, Sarah F. "Women's Unpaid Labor: Home and Community." Pp. 287-301 in *Women Working: Theories and Facts in Perspective*, 2nd ed. edited by Ann Helton Stromberg and Shirley Harkess. Mountain View, Calif.: Mayfield, 1988.

Bielby, William T., and Denise D. Bielby. "Family Ties: Balancing commitments to Work and Family in Dual Earner Households." *American Sociological Review* 54, no. 5 (October 1989): 776-89.

Biggart, Nicole W. *Charismatic Capitalism: Direct Selling Organizations in America*. Chicago: University of Chicago Press, 1989.

Boris, Eileen. "Homework and Women's Rights: The Case of the Vermont

Knitters, 1980-1985." *Signs: Journal of Women in Culture and Society* 13, no. 1 (fall 1987): 98-120.

Brayfield, April A., and Sandra L. Hofferth. "Employment Schedules and Sharing Child Care: Dual-Earner Couples in the United States." Paper presented at the annual meeting of the Southern Sociological Society, Atlanta, Ga., April 1991.

Brett, Jeanne M., and Sara Yogev. "Restructuring Work for Family: How Dual-Earner Couples with Children Manage." Pp. 159-174 in *Work and Family: Theory, Research, and Applications*, edited by Elizabeth B. Goldsmith. Newbury Park, Calif.: Sage Publications, 1989.

Brush, Lisa D. "Gender, Work, Who Cares?! Production, Reproduction, Deindustrialization, and Business as Usual." Pp. 161-189 in *Revisioning Gender*, edited by Myra Marx Ferree, Judith Lorber, and Beth B. Hess. Thousand Oaks, Calif.: Sage Publications, 1999.

Calasanti, Toni M., and Carol A. Bailey. "Gender Inequality and the Division of Household Labor in the United States and Sweden: A Socialist-Feminist Approach." *Social Problems* 38, no. 1 (February 1991): 34-53.

Cancian, Francesca M., and Stacey J. Oliker. *Caring and Gender*. Thousands Oaks, Calif.: Pine Forge Press, 2000.

Carter, Ruth, and Gill Kirkup. *Women in Engineering: A Good Place to Be*. Hampshire, England: MacMillan, 1990.

Chafetz, Janet S. "The Gender Division of Labor and the Reproduction of Female Disadvantage." *Journal of Family Issues* 9, no. 1 (March 1988): 108-131.

Ciucci, William "A la carte . . ." *Richmond Times-Dispatch*, June 10, 2001, K1-2.

Collins, Sheila K. "Women at the Top of Women's Fields: Social Work, Nursing, and Education." Pp. 187-201 in *The Worth of Women's Work: A Qualitative Synthesis*, edited by Anne Statham, Eleanor M. Miller, and Hans O. Mauksch. New York: State University of New York Press, 1988.

Connelly, Maureen, and Patricia Rhoton. "Women in Direct Sales: A Comparison of Mary Kay and Amway Sales Workers." Pp. 245-264 in *The Worth of Women's Work: A Qualitative Synthesis*, edited by Anne Statham, Eleanor M. Miller, and Hans O. Mauksch. New York: State University of New York Press, 1988.

Coverman, Shelley. "Role Overload, Role Conflict, and Stress: Addressing Consequences of Multiple-Role Demands." *Social Forces* 67, no. 3 (June 1989): 965-982.

Daniels, Arlene Kaplan. "Good Times and Good Works: The Place of Sociability in the Work of Women Volunteers." *Social Problems* 32, no. 4 (April 1985): 363-374.

Dryden, Caroline. *Being Married, Doing Gender: A Critical Analysis of Gender Relationships in Marriage.* New York: Routledge, 1999.

Dunn, Dana. "Introduction to the Study of Women and Work." Pp. 1-13 in *Workplace/Women's Place: An Anthology*, edited by Dana Dunn. Los Angeles: Roxbury Publishing Company, 1997.

Epstein, Cynthia Fuchs. *Women in Law.* Garden City, N.Y.: Anchor Books, 1983.

Erikson, Kai. "Introduction." Pp. 1-15 in *The Nature of Work: Sociological Perspectives*, edited by Kai Erikson and Steven P. Vallas. New Haven, Conn.: Yale University Press, 1990.

Feldberg, Roslyn L., and Evelyn N. Glenn. "Male and Female: Job Versus Gender Models in the Sociology of Work." Pp. 65-80 in *Women and Work: Problems and Perspectives*, edited by Rachel Kahn-Hut, Arlene Kaplan Daniels, and Richard Colvard. New York: Oxford University Press, 1982.

Garey, Anita Ilta. *Weaving Work and Motherhood.* Philadelphia, Pa.: Temple University Press, 1999.

Garton-Good, Julie. *Real Estate a la Carte.* Chicago: Dearborn-Kaplan Publishing Company, 2001.

Gerson, Kathleen. *Hard Choices: How Women Decide about Work, Career, and Motherhood.* Berkeley: University of California Press, 1985.

Glenn, Evelyn Nakano. "From Servitude to Service Work: Historical Continuities in the Racial Division of Paid Reproductive Labor." *Signs: Journal of Women in Culture and Society* 18, no. 1 (fall 1992): 1-43.

———. "The Social Construction and Institutionalization of Gender and Race: An Integrative Framework." Pp. 3-43 in *Revisioning Gender*, edited by Myra Marx Ferree, Judith Lorber, and Beth B. Hess. Thousand Oaks, Calif.: Sage Publications, 1999.

Goffman, Erving. *The Presentation of Self in Everyday Life.* New York: Doubleday Anchor Books, 1959.

Harding, Sandra. *The Science Question in Feminism.* Ithaca, N.Y.: Cornell University Press, 1986.

Hawskesworth, Mary. "Confounding Gender." *Signs: Journal of Women in Culture and Society* 22, no. 3 (spring 1997): 649-685.

Hedley, R. Alan. *Making a Living: Technology and Change.* New York: Harper Collins, 1992.

Hickey, Gordon, and David Ress. "Study Cites Prejudice in Housing."

*Richmond Times-Dispatch,* January 12, 1997, A1.

Hochschild, Arlie. *The Managed Heart: Commercialization of Human Feeling.* Berkeley: University of California Press, 1983.

———. *The Second Shift: Working Parents and the Revolution at Home.* New York: Viking Press, 1989.

———. *The Time Bind: When Work Becomes Home and Home Becomes Work.* New York: Metropolitan Books, 1997.

Hodson, Randy, and Teresa A. Sullivan. *The Social Organization of Work.* New York: Wadsworth Publishing Company, 1995.

Hood, Jane C. "The Caretakers: Keeping the Area up and the Family Together." Pp. 93-107 in *The Worth of Women's Work: A Qualitative Synthesis,* edited by Anne Statham, Eleanor M. Miller, and Hans O. Mauksch. Albany: State University of New York Press, 1988.

House, J. D. *Contemporary Entrepreneurs: The Sociology of Residential Real Estate Agents.* Westport, Conn.: Greenwood Press, 1977.

Hughes, Everett C. "A Study of a Secular Institution: The Chicago Real Estate Board." Diss., U of Chicago, 1928.

———. "Work and Self." Pp. 338-347 in *The Sociological Eye: Selected Papers on Work, Self & the Study of Society,* edited by Everett C. Hughes. Chicago: Aldine-Atherton, (1951) 1971.

Hunt, Janet G., and Larry L. Hunt. "Dilemmas and Contradictions of Status: The Case of the Dual-Career Family." *Social Problems* 24, no. 4 (April 1977): 407-416.

———. "The Dualities of Careers and Families: New Integrations or New Polarizations?" *Social Problems* 29, no. 5 (June 1982): 499-510.

———. "Male Resistance to Role Symmetry in Dual-Earner Households: Three Alternative Explanations." Pp. 192-203 in *Families and Work,* edited by Naomi Gerstel and Harriet E. Gross. Philadelphia, Pa.: Temple University Press, 1987.

Judd, Karen, and Sandy M. Pope. "The New Job Squeeze: Women Pushed into Part-Time Work." *Ms. Magazine* 4 (May/June 1994): 86-90.

Jencks, Christopher, Larry Perman, and Lee Rainwater. "What is a Good Job? A New Measure of Labor-Market Success." *American Journal of Sociology* 93, no. 6 (May 1988): 1322-1357.

Kivimaki, Riikka. "Work and Parenthood." Pp. 89-100 in *Gendered Practices in Working Life,* edited by Liisa Rantalaiho and Tuula Heiskanen. New York: St. Martin's Press, 1997.

Lawson, Helene M. *Ladies on the Lot: Women, Car Sales, and the Pursuit of the American Dream.* Lanham, Maryland: Rowman & Littlefield Publishers, 2000.

Leidner, Robin. "Serving Hamburgers and Selling Insurance: Gender, Work, and Identity in Interactive Service Jobs." *Gender & Society* 5, no. 2 (June 1991): 154-177.

———. *Fast Food, Fast Talk: Service Work and the Routinization of Everyday Life*. Berkeley: University of California Press, 1993.

Lorber, Judith. *Paradoxes of Gender*. New Haven, Conn.: Yale University Press, 1994.

Loscocco, Karyn A., and Joyce Robinson. "Barriers to Women's Small-Business Success in the United States." *Gender & Society* 5, no. 4 (December 1991): 511-532.

Martin, Patricia Y., and David L. Collinson. "Gender and Sexuality in Organizations." Pp. 285-310 in *Revisioning Gender*, edited by Myra Marx Ferree, Judith Lorber, and Beth B. Hess Thousand Oaks, Calif.: Sage Publications, 1999.

Mayall, Donald. "Temporary Work and Labor Market Detachment: New Mechanisms and New Opportunities." Pp. 163-192 in *The New Modern Times: Factors Reshaping the World of Work*, edited by David B. Bills, Albany: State University of New York Press, 1995.

McIlwee, Judith S., and J. Gregg Robinson. *Women in Engineering: Gender, Power, and Workplace Culture*. New York: State University of New York Press, 1992.

Meara, Hannah. "Honor in Dirty Work: The Case of American Meat Cutters and Turkish Butchers." *Sociology of Work and Occupations* 1, no. 3 (August 1974): 259-283.

Miller, Jeanne, and Howard H. Garrison. "Sex Roles: The Division of Labor at Home and in the Workplace." *Annual Review of Sociology*, vol. 8 (1982): 237-262.

National Association of Realtors, "The Data Bank." *NAR Members Survey 1999*. http://www.nar.REALTOR.com/research/papers/member.html (January 11, 2000).

Nippert-Eng, Christena E. *Home and Work: Negotiating Boundaries through Everyday Life*. Chicago: University of Chicago Press, 1996.

Padavic, Irene. "White Collar Work Values and Women's Interest in Blue-Collar Jobs." *Gender & Society* 6, no. 2 (June 1992): 215-230.

Paules, Greta Foff. *Dishing it Out: Power and Resistance among Waitresses in a New Jersey Restaurant*. Philadelphia, Pa.: Temple University Press, 1991.

Phelan, Jo, Evelyn J. Bromet, Joseph E. Schwartz, Mary Amanda Dew, and E. Carroll Curtis. "The Work Environments of Male and Female Professionals." *Sociology of Work and Occupations* 20, no.1 (February

1993): 68-89.

Polivka, Anne E., and Thomas Nardone. "On the Definition of 'Contingent Work.'" *Monthly Labor Review* 112, no. 12 (December 1989): 9-16.

Presser, Harriet B. "Shift Work and Child Care Among Young Dual-Earner American Parents." *Journal of Marriage and the Family* 50, no.1 (February 1988): 133-148.

Pringle, Rosemary. *Secretaries Talk: Sexuality, Power and Work.* London: Verso, 1989.

Reskin, Barbara F., and Patricia A. Roos. *Job Queues, Gender Queues: Explaining Women's Inroads into Male Occupations.* Philadelphia, Pa.: Temple University Press, 1990.

Reskin, Barbara F., and Irene Padavic. *Women and Men at Work.* Thousand Oaks, Calif.: Pine Forge Press, 1994.

Richmond Association of Realtors. "Study Shows What Top Producers Look for When Selecting a Firm." *The Richmond Association of Realtors* (December 1996): 9.

Ritzer, George. *Sociological Beginnings: On the Origins of Key Ideas in Sociology.* New York: McGraw-Hill, 1994.

Romero, Mary. *Maid in the U.S.A.* New York: Routledge, Chapman, and Hall, 1992.

Rosen, Ellen I. *Bitter Choices: Blue-Collar Women in and out of Work.* Chicago: University of Chicago Press, 1989.

Rothman, Sheila M., and Emily Menlo Marks. "Adjusting Work and Family Life: Flexible Work Schedules and Family Policy." Pp. 469-477 in *Families and Work*, edited by Naomi Gerstel and Harriet Engel Gross. Philadelphia, Pa.: Temple University Press, 1987.

Schor, Juliet B. *The Overworked American.* New York: Basic Books, 1991.

Schwartz, Felice N. *Breaking with Tradition: Women and Work, The New Facts of Life.* New York: Warner Books, 1992.

Shelton, Beth Anne. "The Distribution of Household Tasks: Does Wife's Employment Make a Difference?" *Journal of Family Issues* 11, no. 2 (June 1990): 115-135.

Smith, Dorothy E. "Women's Inequality and the Family." Pp. 23-54 in *Families and Work*, edited by Naomi Gerstel and Harriet Engel Gross. Philadelphia, Pa.: Temple University Press, 1987.

———. *The Everyday World as Problematic: A Feminist Sociology.* Boston: Northeastern University Press, 1987.

Statham, Anne, Eleanor M. Miller, and Hans O. Mauksch. "The Integration Work: A Second-Order Analysis of Qualitative Research." Pp. 11-35 in *The Worth of Women's Work: A Qualitative Synthesis*, edited by Anne

Statham, Eleanor M. Miller, and Hans O. Mauksch, Albany: State University of New York Press. 1988.

Strober, Myra H. "Toward a General Theory of Occupational Sex Segregation: The Case of Public School Teaching." Pp. 144-156 in *Sex Segregation in the Workplace: Trends, Explanations, Remedies*, edited by Barbara F. Reskin. Washington, D.C.: National Academy Press, 1984.

Thomas, Barbara J., and Barbara F. Reskin. "A Woman's Place is Selling Homes: Occupational Change and the Feminization of Real Estate Sales." Pp. 205-223 in *Job Queues, Gender Queues: Explaining Women's Inroads into Male Occupations*, edited by Barbara F. Reskin and Patricia A. Roos. Philadelphia, Pa.: Temple University Press, 1990.

Wallace, Ruth A. "Catholic Women and the Creation of a New Social Reality." *Gender & Society* 2, no. 1 (March 1988): 24-38.

Weston, Kath. "Production as Means, Production as Metaphor: Women's Struggles to Enter the Trades." Pp. 137-151 in *Uncertain Terms: Negotiating Gender in American Culture*, edited by Faye Ginsburg and Anna Lowenhaupt Tsing. Boston: Beacon Press, 1990.

Wharton, Carol S. "Finding Time for the 'Second Shift': The Impact of Flexible Work Schedules on Women's Double Days." *Gender & Society* 8, no. 2 (June 1994): 189-205.

———. "Making People Feel Good: Workers' Constructions of Meaning in Interactive Service Jobs." *Qualitative Sociology* 19, no. 2 (summer 1996): 217-234.

———. "From Casuals to Careers: The Professionalization of Real Estate Saleswork." Pp. 115-134 in *Current Research on Occupations and Professions. Jobs in Context: Circles and Settings*, vol. 10, edited by Helena Z. Lopata. Greenwich, Conn.: Jai Press, 1998.

Wilensky, Harold L. "The Professionalization of Everyone?" *American Journal of Sociology* 70, no. 2 (September 1965): 137-158.

# Index

administrative work, 128. *See also* paperwork
advertising, 38, 45–46, 51, 128
African American women, 8, 59–60. *See also* blacks
agencies, 9–10. *See also* company(ies)
agent luncheons, 52
Allen, Ginger, 27, 44, 71–72
altruism and autonomy, 25
Amway (direct sales organization), 42
anxiety, 128. *See also* stress
attractiveness, of work, 12
autonomy, 7, 120, 138, 139; and altruism, 25; of contingent work, 32; and home-work boundaries, 7; and job choice, 121–22, 124; and job satisfaction, 119, 139; in work schedule, 20, 21

babysitters for children, 72, 78, 94. *See also* day-care
Barnes, Nadia, 59
Barnes, Sandra, 46
benefit policies, 21, 22, 23, 129, 134

Berry, Sandra, 40, 57, 69, 71, 78; on family responsibilities, 87, 92, 96; on gender bias, 110; on paperwork, 127
Bird, Elaine, 125, 127
black clients, 59
blacks and integration, 30
black women, 8. *See also* African American women
boundaries, home and work, 7, 20–21, 70, 95–98; and family obligations, 12, 84, 95–97; and personal preference, 78–79, 133; weaving of, 5–6, 133, 134, 139
brokers/managers, 22, 86, 101, 123; and commission, 44, 45; licensing of, 25, 38; men as, 28, 30; and realtor retention, 23
Burns, Casey, 1, 104
buyer's agent, 56. *See also* clients/customers

caravanning, 52, 57
car expenses, 47
casual labor, 23. *See also* contingent labor
Century 21 (franchise firm), 24, 30

Certified Residential Specialist (CRS), 25
Certified Site Agent (CSA), 25, 27
challenges, 123
Chicago Real Estate Board, 23
*Chicago Tribune* (newspaper), 28
children, 6, 83–84; care of, 9, 85, 88–89, 94, 136; household work of, 88; latch-key, 14n18; paid care for, 72, 78, 93–94; school events of, 85. *See also* family obligations
class, 8, 124; and race, 4, 57–60. *See also* middle class; status
clerical work, 29–30. *See also* paper work
clients/customers, 49–53; and agent's self-presentation, 62–63; defined, 64n13; difficult, 123; and disclosure form, 55–56; and emotion work, 22, 55, 107–8, 125–27, 135; farming for, 50–51; and gender, 107–10, 137; loyalty of, 56, 126, 132n19; and market niche, 53–57; out of town referrals, 52–53; positive interactions with, 124, 135; preferences of, 58; previewing homes for, 56–57; and routinization, 32; and seasonal weather, 68; and service work, 20, 21, 132n18; and working hours, 76, 134
code of ethics, 25, 26, 27, 59, 135
college education, 9, 121–22
Collinson, David L., 102
commercial sales, 30, 31, 112–14
commissions, 23, 43–47, 68, 117; and computerization, 62; and expenses, 52, 128; and independent contractors, 24, 29, 43, 47, 134; and professionalism, 136; for site agents, 38, 57
company(ies): affiliation with, 11, 23, 38–42, 134; and compensation, 43, 44, 45; customer strategies of, 52–53; dot.coms, 60-61; national franchises, 9–10, 24, 30, 44; reputation of, 46; and training, 22
compatibility, 86–87
compensation, 22, 26; negotiating of, 42–47. *See also* commissions; income
computers, 20, 60–63
conceptual territories, 7
Conley, Roger, 61
contingent work, 11, 21–22, 32, 129
customers. *See* clients/customers
CyberHomes.com, 60
cyberselling, 60–63

day-care for children, 72, 78, 93–94
Denton, Ellie, 107–8, 128–29
desegregation, 3, 30
direct sales work, 3
direct selling organizations (DSOs), 42, 103, 120
"dirty work," 126, 127
disability pay, 21, 22
disclosure form, 55–56
discrimination, 60, 110–11. *See also* race and class; resegregation; occupational stereotypes
divorce/separation, 83, 84, 92–93, 97
domestic responsibility, 72. *See also* family obligations
domestic workers, 85, 93–94
dot.coms, 60–61
drawbacks (piques), 124–29
Dryden, Carolyn, 89
DSOs. *See* direct selling organizations

economy, 68. *See also* market
education, 39, 120, 138; college, 9, 121–22; gender resegregation in, 29. *See also* training
electronic (e-)mail, 20, 62
emotional downsizing, 97
emotional labor, 11, 95, 123, 124, 129; and clients, 22, 55, 107–8,

125–27, 135; and job choice, 119, 120, 139
emotional support and family, 92–93, 97
employee benefits, 21, 22, 23, 129, 134
employer-employee relationship, 23, 32, 139. *See also* brokers/managers
Engels, Deborah, 43, 54, 73, 121; on family obligations, 96–97; on procurring clients, 51
entrepreneurs, 21, 24. *See also* independent contractors
entry requirements, 24, 27, 120, 121–22. *See also* education; licensing; training
Erikson, Kai, 133
ethics, code of, 25, 26, 27, 59, 135
ethnicity, 59. *See also* race
Evans, Inez, 122
evening work, 69, 71, 75, 127, 134–35
Ewing, Colleen, 94, 123
expenses, compensation for, 45–46, 47, 52, 128–29

family obligations, 2–3, 20, 83–100, 133; and childcare, 9, 83–84, 85, 88–89, 94, 136; and compatibility, 86–87, 119–20; and division of labor, 85; and domestic workers, 85, 93; and household division of labor, 85, 87, 88–89, 91–92, 136; and job sharing at home, 88–93; male (husband) role in, 5, 85, 87, 88–93; and phone work, 94–95, 96, 136; and reduced work load, 72; weaving work with, 5–6, 134; and workday, 75–76, 79; and work-home boundaries, 12, 84, 95–97; and work hours, 86–87
"farming" for clients, 50–51

*Fast Food, Fast Talk: Service Work and the Routinization of Everyday Life* (Leidner), 33n10, 34n31, 37
fee-for-service, 47
feminine organizations, 103. *See also* direct selling organizations
femininity, 102, 114. *See also* gender; women
feminization, occupational, 118
FIZBOs. *See* For Sale By Owner
flexibility in work, 127, 139; and family obligations, 84–85, 86–87, 89–90; and home and work boundaries, 12, 95, 134; and job choice, 120–21, 124; scheduling, 7, 67, 86–87, 89–90, 122–23, 136
Foote, Allison, 77, 108–9, 124–25
For Sale By Owner (FIZBOs), 26, 51
franchises, national, 9–10, 24, 30, 44

Garey, Anita Ilta, 5, 139
Garton-Good, Julie, 47
gender, 7, 12, 32, 101–16, 124; and agent's self-presentation, 63, 111; as asset, 106–9; and compensation, 44–45, 139; composition in residential sales, 28–31; construction of, 102, 104, 114, 137; as difference, 111–12; and family obligations, 84, 133, 136; and flexibility, 123; identity, 102, 106, 111, 114; ideology of, 91–92; and labor queues, 119; as liability, 109–11; and occupational resegregation, 2, 3, 29, 31, 137–38; organizing by, 104–6; as placement, 112–14; stereotypes, 108, 112, 113; and work experience, 4–5
ghettoization, 31
Gibson, Jennifer, 58, 113–14
Goffman, Irving, 62
Gordon, Jennifer, 90–91, 93
Graduate Realtor® Institute (GRI), 27

Gray, Vicky, 74–75, 76
Greene, Gillian, 90

Habitat for Humanity, 25
"halo effect" of work, 124
Harden, Chris, 111, 122
hard work, 49
health care/insurance, 21, 22, 46, 134
"high touch" occupations, 20, 62. *See also* emotional work; interactive service work
Hochschild, Arlie, 14n18, 84, 88, 97
HomeAdvisor.com, 60
home and office, 77. *See also* office
home and work boundaries. *See* boundaries, home and work
Homebytes.com, 61
HomeSeekers.com, 60
home seller/buyer, 21, 53–55. *See also* clients/customers
HomeShark.com, 61
HomeStore.com, 61
Horner, Karen, 113
hours worked. *See* workday; working hours
House, J. D., 24, 132n19
household labor, 85, 87, 88–89, 93–95, 136. *See also* family obligations
housing market, 22, 68–69, 71. *See also* market
Howell, Laura, 91, 105–6, 108
Hughes, Everett C., 23, 28
husbands and family, 5, 85, 87, 88–93. *See also* masculinity; men

ideal salesperson, 86, 97
identity: and agent's self-presentation, 63, 124; and gender, 102, 106, 111, 114
image of realtors, 27
income, 73, 120, 121–22, 134, 139; disatisfaction with, 128–29; husband's, 91; negotiating, 43–48. *See also* commissions

income taxes, 22, 129
independent contractors, 11, 40; autonomy of, 25, 32, 124; commission work of, 24, 29, 43, 47, 134; contingent status of, 21–22, 129; customer strategies of, 53–54; long hours of, 72; self-motivation of, 49; and work schedule, 67. *See also* self-employment
industrialization and work-home boundaries, 7
information processing, 19
insurance, 22, 23, 46, 134
interactive service work, 11, 22, 37, 120; and client, 21, 126, 130, 135; and self-presentation, 63
Internal Revenue Service (IRS), 42, 129. *See also* taxes
Internet, 20, 60–63
interviewees (participants), 8–11. *See also specific interviewees*

Jacobs, Judith, 117, 123–24
James, Elaine, 39, 41, 49, 50–51, 74
Jefferson, Patrice, 69–70, 71, 77
job choice, 120, 138, 139; and queuing model, 117, 118–19
job dissatisfaction, 124–29, 130, 138
job history, 9
job model and gender, 5
*Job Queues, Gender Queues: Explaining Women's Inroads into Male Occupations* (Reskin and Roos), 117, 137–38
job security, 22, 23, 139; and computerization, 61–62
Jones, Kendra, 73–74, 83, 97, 126; on gender difference, 91–92, 112

Kight, Lana, 45–46, 67, 76
Kivimaki, Riikka, 83

labor demand, 29. *See also* job;work
labor shortage, 119

Lange, Cara, 39–40, 52, 53, 55, 61
latch-key children, 14n18
Leidner, Robin, 32, 33n10, 34n31, 37, 49
licensing, 38, 40; by state, 25, 27, 135; and training, 22, 135
life insurance, 22
listing *vs.* site agent, 57
Loomis, Andrea, 128
Lorber, Judith, 101
loyalty, buyer's, 56, 126, 132n19

McCain, Drew, 72
managers. *See* brokers/managers
marital relations, 89; divorce/separation, 83, 84, 92–93, 97. *See also* family obligations
market: conditions of, 48–49; establishing niche in, 53–57; housing, 68–69, 71
marketing: electronic, 60–63; expenses of, 46. *See also* advertising
Marks, Tonia, 27, 46, 88, 90, 92; on college education, 121–22; on company affiliation, 40–41, 42; on phone work, 94–95, 96; on previewing homes, 57; on race blindness, 59
Martin, Patricia Y., 102
Mary Kay Cosmetics, 42, 47, 103, 120
masculinity: and agent's self-presentation, 63; corporate model of, 102–3; and work experience, 4, 113. *See also* gender; men
Mayall, Donald, 19
medical insurance/leave, 21, 139
men: as agents, and women compared, 107–9, 137; as brokers, 28; and commercial sales, 30, 112–14; in education, 29; family obligations of, 5, 84, 85, 88–93; gender bias of, 109–11; and residential sales, 30–31; and women's organizations, 104, 105; and work experience, 4, 30. *See also* gender; masculinity
Mendenhall, Richard, 62
middle class, 29, 139
middle-class women, 3, 4
Miller, Fiona, 71, 104–5
minorities, 3, 4. *See also* African American women; race and class
MLS. *See* Multiple Listings Services
mommy track, 5. *See also* family obligations
motivation, 49, 110, 119
*Ms.* magazine, 103
Multiple Listing Services (MLS), 38, 41, 46, 51, 60–61
National Association of Bank Women (NABW), 105
National Association of Realtors (NAR), 25, 26, 38, 41, 61–62; member survey by, 8–9, 44, 45
national franchises, 9–10, 24, 30, 44
*The Nature of Work: Sociological Perspectives* (Erikson), 133
networking, 104–6
Nippert-Eng, Christena, 7

occupational feminization, 118
occupational placement, 117–18. *See also* job choice
occupational resegregation, 2, 3, 29, 30, 137–38
occupational tipping, 3
office, 23, 77–79; expenses, 45, 46; shopping mall kiosk, 76–77
old-boy network, 104
open houses, 51–52, 57, 75, 78
opportunity and job choice, 118
organization, 11–13; and gender, 104–6
orientation model, 5
out-of-town referrals, 52–53
overwork, 67
*The Overworked American* (Schor), 67

paperwork, 69–70, 73, 74, 125, 127–28 clerical work, 29-30
*Paradoxes of Gender* (Lorber), 101
para-professional work, 3
parenthood, 84. *See also* children
participants (interviewees), 8–11. *See also specific interviewees*
pay structure. *See* commissions; compensation; income
people services, 20, 123. *See also* emotion work; interactive service work
perquisites, 120–24
personal contact, 62, 95
personal preference, 78–79, 133
personal time, 70, 73, 75
phone work, 51, 70, 78–79; and family obligations, 94–95, 96, 134, 136; and workday, 73, 74, 75
piques (drawbacks), 124–29; paperwork, 69–70, 73, 74, 125, 127–28. *See also* emotional labor
power-brokering, 124
prejudice, 111. *See also* discrimination
previewing homes, 56–57
professionalization, 24–27, 38, 105, 135–36, 137
pseudo-profession, 11
public perception, 27, 126; and professionalism, 25, 135
pyramid schemes, 42

queuing model, 117, 118–19

race, 8, 30; and class, 4, 57–60
racism, 59. *See also* discrimination
real estate agencies, 10
*Real Estate a la Carte* (Garton-Good), 47
Realtor®, 8, 25, 38, 60
REALTOR.COM, 60
recruitment, 23
redlining (discriminatory practice), 59, 60

referrals, client, 51, 52–53
rejection, 126
research, 10–11
resegregation, by gender, 2, 3, 29, 30, 137–38
residential sales: gender composition in, 28–31, 107–9, 112; *vs.* commercial sales, 112–14
residential tipping, 3
Reskin, Barbara F., 1, 117, 118; on resegregation, 2, 3, 30–31, 137
retirement/pension fund, 21, 46, 128, 134, 138
Rice, Pamela, 37, 52–53, 54, 58–59, 78
Rivers, Elizabeth, 48, 49, 101
Roos, Patricia A., 2, 3, 30–31, 137; on job queues, 117, 118
routinization of work, 31–32

sales commission. *See* commissions
sales volume, 47–49
scheduling work, 12, 67–68, 73–77; autonomy in, 20, 21; flexibility in, 7, 67, 86–87, 89–90, 122–23, 136; and household labor, 85, 86
school events, 85
Schor, Juliet B., 67, 68
scripting of work, 31–32
seasonal weather cycles, 68
segregation. *See* resegregation gender
self-employment, 21, 120, 123. *See also* independent contractors
self-esteem, 126
self-identity, 124. *See also* identity
self-motivation, 49, 119
self-presentation, 62–63, 111
seniority, 71
service provision, 19–20
service work, 3, 132n18, 139. *See also* interactive service work
shopping mall kiosk, 76–77
sick leave, 21. *See also* health care
site *vs.* listing agent, 57
skilled trades, 4

Sloan, Heather, 70–71, 75, 77–78, 89
snowball sampling, 8
socialization, 95, 102, 118, 137
social security, 21, 22, 46, 128, 134, 138
societal expectations, 137
socioeconomic stratification, 58. *See also* class; status
state licensing, 25, 27, 135
status: and professionalism, 24, 25–26, 27; and self-presentation, 62–63, 124
steering (discriminatory practice), 60
stereotypes: gender, 108, 112, 113; of woman realtor, 28, 105
Stewart, Erika, 120
stress, 96, 125, 137

Tax Equity and Fiscal Responsibility Act (TEFRA) of 1982, 43, 45
taxes, 21, 22, 23, 43, 129
teaching professions, 29
technological changes, 19–20, 62, 94. *See also* computers
telecommunications, 20. *See also* phone work
temporary (casual) work, 21, 23. *See also* contingent work
"Temporary Work and Labor Market Detachment: New Mechanisms and New Opportunties" (Mayall), 19
Thomas, Barbara J., 1
*The Time Bind: When Work Becomes Home and Home Becomes Work* (Hochschild), 97
time poverty, 67, 127. *See also* scheduling; workday
tipping, 3
training, 12, 22, 26, 135, 138; and company connection, 39; and licensing, 25, 135; and routinization, 32; standards of, 27–28; techniques of, 34n31. *See also* education

Tripp, Beth, 19, 48, 54, 126, 133; on gender bias, 109, 111
Tupperware (corporation), 103, 120
turnover rate, 41, 130

unemployment insurance, 21
unpredictability in work, 123, 128, 129

vacation pay, 21, 23, 138
Virginia real estate board, 43
voice mail, 20, 94. *See also* phone work

wages, 29. *See also* commission; income
weaving metaphor, 5–6, 133, 134, 139. *See also* boundaries, home and work
web pages, 41. *See also* Internet
weekend work, 69, 71, 127; and client's needs, 134–35; open houses, 75, 78
White, Tess, 75–76, 86–87, 91, 93, 127; on gender difference, 108, 111
white collar work, 3
white flight, 30
Willis, Katherine, 10
"A Woman's Place is Selling Homes" (Thomas and Reskin), 1
women: African American, 8, 59–60; as contingent workers, 22; and emotional labor, 124; and occupational feminization, 118; and work, 3–7; work opportunities for, 119–20. *See also* femininity; gender
Women's Council of Realtors (WCR), 104–6
women's work, 3, 28
word-of-mouth referrals, 51
work: changing nature of, 19–20; routinization/scripting of, 31–32;

and women, 3–7. *See also* interactive service work
work and family, 9, 83. *See also* family obligations
work and home boundaries. *See* boundaries, home and work
"Work and Parenthood" (Kivimaki), 83
workday, 67–79; and boundary issues, 70; evenings, 69, 71, 75, 127, 134–35; and family obligations, 72, 76; and housing market, 71–72; office, 77–79; paperwork in, 69–70, 73, 74; personal time in, 70, 73, 75; phone work in, 74, 75; scheduling of, 67–68, 73–77
workers, 124; and job queues, 117, 118–19
working class women, 4
working father, 5
working hours, 43, 134–35; and family obligations, 86–87, 136; flexibility in, 84–85, 120–21, 122, 127; and seniority, 71. *See also* weekend work; workday
working mother, 5
workmen's compensation, 21
work pattern, 12. *See also* scheduling
workplace culture, 103
"work smart," 58

## About the Author

Carol S. Wharton is an Associate Professor of Sociology and Women's Studies at the University of Richmond, Virginia. Her research interests focus on the interrelationship of gender, work, and family, and how the arrangements women make to accommodate each sphere change over the life course. She received her Ph.D. in sociology from Michigan State University.